# THE DRAMA OF THE
# GIFTED CHILD

# THE
# DRAMA
## OF THE GIFTED
# CHILD

## The Search for the True Self

*Completely Revised and Updated
With a New Introduction by the Author*

# Alice Miller
### TRANSLATED BY RUTH WARD

**BasicBooks**
*A Division of HarperCollinsPublishers*

A previous version of chapter 1 appeared in the *International Journal of Psychoanalysis* 60 (1979): 47; a previous version of chapter 2 appeared in the *International Review of Psychoanalysis* 6 (1979): 61; a previous version of the appendix appeared as the afterword to Alice Miller, *For Your Own Good*, 2nd ed. (New York: Farrar, Straus & Giroux, 1984).

Grateful acknowledgment is made for permission to reprint excerpts from the following: Hermann Hesse, "A Child's Heart," from *Klingsor's Last Summer*, translated by Richard and Clara Winston (New York: Farrar, Straus and Giroux, 1970), and *Demian*, translated by Michael Roloff and Michael Lebeck (New York: Harper & Row, 1965).

*Designed by Ellen Levine*

Library of Congress Cataloging-in-Publication Data
Miller, Alice.
    [Drama des begabten Kindes. English]
    The drama of the gifted child : the search for the true self /
Alice Miller ; translated by Ruth Ward. — Completely rev. & updated.
    p.   cm.
    Includes bibliographical references and index
    Originally published: Prisoners of childhood.
    ISBN 0–465–01694–4. — ISBN 0–465–01693–6 (pbk.)
    1. Narcissism.  2. Self-esteem.  3. Psychology, Pathological.
I. Title.
RC553.N36M5413  1994
616.89—dc20
                                              94–8333
                                             CIP

94 95 96 97 ◆/HC 9 8 7 6 5 4 3 2 1

# Contents

# Acknowledgments

I FIRST want to express my profound gratitude to my editor, Premi Pearson, whose invaluable assistance actually made this revision possible. Premi's deep understanding of the material, her precision, clarity, and honesty in thinking—based on her own experience and her respect for the experience of others— came like a precious, quite unexpected gift to me. We have never met, and throughout the editing process we have been separated by eight hours of time difference; we have even had to deal with manuscripts lost in the Christmas mail. Yet this was the most perfect collaboration I have ever had the opportunity to enjoy. Premi's questions and suggestions not only helped me express myself more clearly in English, but her genuine interest and emotional understanding of the issues often motivated me to say more than I had originally intended. I believe this has been in the reader's best interest.

Fortunately, once at Basic Books, the manuscript received the personal attention of Jo Ann Miller, who was very sensitive and considerate in regard to the comprehensive changes the *Drama* has had to endure. Thanks to her vivid interest in the Four-Step Method, this effective system of self-therapy has been elaborated within this revision more extensively than I had originally intended. I am very grateful for her suggestions, interest, and help.

My gratitude for J. Konrad Stettbacher's discovery must also be mentioned here, although it is already expressed in many pages of this book. On a very personal level, I want to say that without having undergone this therapy, I would hardly have had either the wish or the energy and clarity to undertake this revision. I certainly could not have done it with so much pleasure and engagement or have finished it in such a short time.

Not least, I would like to thank all of the readers who have written to me since 1979 and who continue to write and tell me what they have discovered about their lives. Many have sent me material and information that has opened my eyes about various important issues. It was difficult not always to be able to answer each letter personally. I hope that many of you will recognize in this revision my answer to you, as well as my gratitude and sense of obligation.

# THE DRAMA OF THE GIFTED CHILD

# Introduction to the Revised Edition (1994)

O<small>VER</small> the years, I have been reluctant to make any revisions in my first three books—*The Drama of the Gifted Child, For Your Own Good,* and *Thou Shalt Not Be Aware*—because I did not wish to disguise my own life history. But today this wish has taken second place to others that, in view of the enormous readership of the *Drama,* now seem more important. Most of my readers find themselves confronting their own life histories as they read my books, and I did not want an anachronistic language to stand in the way of that encounter. This book was written sixteen years ago in keeping with the precepts of psychoanalysis, precepts that I have long since moved beyond and today regard as misleading. I therefore have had to revise the text thoroughly, salvaging those parts I still regard as valid and useful while clarifying certain points more than I was able to in 1978.

Since the publication of the *Drama,* many people have written to me saying that they can trace the moment of their own personal awakening to their reading of the book. It seems to have given them the key to long locked doors, behind which lay the path to their own life histories. Pent-up tears could finally be wept. The strength and similarity of these reactions, despite the diversity of the cultures in which they originated, made it clear to me that the *Drama* touched upon a universal human tragedy that could not be traced exclusively to Western civilization. I also came to see that this tragedy could not be undone in a single generation.

The tragedy is that of early psychic injuries and their inevitable repression, which allows the child to survive. In a broad sense, it is the tragedy of almost everyone: As children we strive, above all else, to accommodate our parents' demands—spoken and unspoken, reasonable and unreasonable. In the process, we blind ourselves to our true needs and feelings. In our adult lives, this is like trying to sail a ship without a compass. Not knowing who we are, what we feel, and what we need, even as grown-ups we remain subject to the expectations placed upon us from the very beginning of our lives, expectations we fulfilled not for love but for the illusion of love. Without that illusion, we could not have survived childhood.

Sadly, the situation has changed little for today's children. The strong—indeed, growing—interest in the *Drama* proves as much. What has changed are the avenues available to adults to resolve their problems. Today anyone who is motivated can have access to a truly effective method of self-therapy.

The original version of the *Drama* did not contain a coherent method of therapy, much less one that people could practice by themselves. It critiqued psychoanalytic practice, while expressing the hope that it would one day be able to remedy the repression of feeling and memory. This hope has once and for all proved to be an illusion. Indeed, psychoanalysis was specifically created by Freud to conceal childhood injuries, and it continues to serve its purpose well.

Freud dealt with his fear of his childhood traumas by making endless unverifiable speculations, and by denying the possibility of a verifiable access to childhood reality. By doing so, he retarded progress in our knowledge of ourselves, and in effective therapeutic work, for a hundred years. Out of his renunciation of the truth he created dogma. Around the question of child abuse and its consequences, he wove a strict taboo. In psychoanalytic circles, one was obliged to accept the credo that psychic illness had its origins in "instinctual conflicts." Everyone, including the most famous analysts such as Spitz, Balint, Winnicott, Kohut, and others (but not John Bowlby) complied with this taboo. As a result, they could not bring to fruition the discovery of child mistreatments they made in their work. And as they did not have the courage to move beyond the framework of psychoanalysis, they sacrificed the truth for their positions within the Psychoanalytic Association. Sandor Ferenczi, who insisted on the validity of his own experience with patients, was ostracized and branded psychotic.

C. G. Jung, though he did dare to break with Freud, took refuge from his own concrete life history in a world of symbols and suppositions. This decision would not have had any consequences for others if it had remained Jung's private business. But Jung disguised his fear with the help of theories that are still held in high esteem by his followers. His ideas are used today to treat disturbed people in a misleading and dangerous way—people who are told, for instance, that violence is a normal part of our nature, a part of our "shadow," and that we only must learn to "deal with it." With such wisdom the confused drug addict and criminal must become even more confused and

violent, because he is being betrayed once again. For it is only
the suppression of justified rage in childhood that makes a person violent and blind. Nothing else. But to admit this fact
would mean to recognize the failures of parents who once (more
or less violently) suppressed this rage. If the Jungian "therapist"
fears his own parents more than anything else, he uses Jung's
theories to sidestep the truth and feels supported in so doing by
the whole Jungian community, based on its master's authority. I
insist on disclosing the roots of this "therapeutic" mistreatment,
because the damage caused by them is enormous and yet
absolutely *avoidable* as soon as the truth can be faced.

Similar "solutions" to personal dilemmas at the expense of
patients and students can be found among other recalcitrants,
like Wilhelm Reich, who went on to found their own school of
thought. I discuss them in my books (see Miller 1984, 1990b,
1991). Had Freud kept faith with the facts, such distortions of
the truth over the last hundred years could never have been
possible. Sadly, the price for such evasions has always been paid
by the patients. They, of course, do not know that psychoanalysis is ultimately a system of defenses, bolstered by appropriate
theories, whose real purpose is the avoidance, not the revela-
tion, of painful truths. The countless letters I have received in
the last twelve years confirm my own experience that psychoanalytical practice serves to cement, not resolve, damage caused
in childhood.

The description of the method that gave me what I had been
seeking throughout my life—namely, an approach to self-
knowledge by which my own life history would be revealed to
me—has now been published in many languages, so that many
people have already been able to help themselves by applying it
(see Stettbacher, 1991). This self-therapy method, enacted in
four steps, is devoted solely to the truth and therefore dispenses
with all mystification and ideology. To repair the damage

caused by early injuries, we must face the truth with our minds and our hearts, acknowledging the pain and fear to which we were subjected. We must speak out against this mistreatment, confronting our parents in an inner dialogue, and we must finally discover and validate our real needs, past and present.

The four steps can be adapted by reading Stettbacher's book. I can here only try to indicate very incompletely their direction: describing precisely your perception of the situation here and now, feeling and articulating your feelings as well as postulating your right to them, seeking and identifying realities, and finally formulating your needs. The four steps will be described in another context in the Afterword. As Stettbacher's concept is based on a discovery of a natural law, the effectiveness of his method depends on accuracy and precision in using the four steps. For that reason I am reluctant to simplify them more than I am doing here.

The repression of injuries endured during childhood is the root cause of psychic disorders and criminality. The price of repression and denial in childhood, however necessary to the child, is the symptoms of the adult. A difficult childhood, even the most cruel, doesn't automatically create a criminal. Taking examples like Hitler, Stalin, and others, I could prove that it was not the cruel childhood alone but rather the total denial of this suffering and the flight from it into destructive grandiosity that drove them to become mass murderers. Thanks to the method developed by Stettbacher, we now know that and we also know how repression can be resolved, namely, via the release of feelings that became blocked at the time of the original trauma. During this process, the unconscious memories of repressed events, which often drive a person to destructive actions, can be transformed into conscious memories that remain available to us in the future and allow us to fulfill our real needs in a peaceful way. The blind acting-out comes then to an end.

The Swiss psychotherapist J. K. Stettbacher was able to develop his remarkably effective therapy method because, unlike Freud and thousands of his successors, he never allowed himself to be deterred by the truth about childhood abuse and neglect and their consequences. As he has written, "For me, making sense of suffering means resolving it. It means seeking and establishing what it is that causes us to suffer today, in order to be able to avoid it in the future." Stettbacher's entire therapeutic project is grounded in this endeavor to lay bare psychic injuries from the remote past in order to be free of their consequences in the present.

Stettbacher describes the crucial mechanism of transference and how to monitor its effects within us. He gives guidance in using the confrontation with ourselves and important others to establish the healing, enlightening dialogue that could never take place before. He explains why it is absolutely essential to voice previously repressed natural needs during therapy, so that we can proceed to fulfill them. One of the fundamental differences between Stettbacher's method and all other forms of therapy known to me is that we are here offered a full account of the dynamics of psychic processes, an account that can be verified by each and every one of us.

The act of reading about these dynamics is itself preparation for therapy and self-help. The description of the therapy shows how we can make available to consciousness feelings and perceptions that have previously been blocked. It shows us how they can be comprehended, integrated, and resolved by means of the Four-Step Method.

To assume that we are dealing here with a special form of Janov's theory, where just feelings are called therapy, would be completely misleading. Stettbacher's concept is entirely different from all therapy methods I know at the moment, and I consider it an undisputed worldwide novelty. People undergoing this therapy not only help themselves but are true pioneers, helping others to learn from their exploration about unnoticed, often unconscious, psychic and physical assaults on children—a knowledge that our "collective unconsciousness" has kept secret for thousands of years. These adults will no longer have to escape from something that happened a long time ago, because they no longer have to deny the fact that what is so hard to believe did actually happen.

Our true, repressed life history is stored up in our body, which attempts to recount it and to be listened to, by way of symptoms. This is in fact for our own well-being, as denial is highly destructive to the adult. Demands to forgive and other moral issues do not reach our cells; they cannot fool them. Cells can, indeed, be manipulated and betrayed by drugs over a certain period of time. In the long run, however, they can only cope with the truth. As soon as the truth can be slowly explored, thanks to the conscious experience of once-repressed feelings, the language of symptoms becomes superfluous. They simply disappear.

I have described the path to my new insights in *Pictures of a Childhood* (1986), *The Untouched Key* (1990), *Banished Knowledge* (1990), and *Breaking Down the Wall of Silence* (1991). In 1988, I officially broke away from psychoanalysis by resigning from the Swiss and the International psychoanalytical associations. My first three books, originally published in Germany between 1979 and 1981, mark the beginning of this development, for it was only as I was writing them that I began systematically to explore childhood, including my own. Thanks to my work on those books, and later to the success of the carefully and systematically revealing therapy, I could see what, despite my critical attitude toward the drive theory, had remained concealed from me during the twenty years of my analytical practice. It was not easy to escape from the labyrinth of psychoanalysis. It took me fifteen years to accomplish this liberation process: from 1973, when spontaneous painting allowed me vaguely to sense the truth, until 1988, when I was finally able to articulate it completely.

For those who are reading my work for the first time, I would like briefly to address several theoretical and practical issues.

According to prehistorians, humans coexisted peacefully for five million years. Had this not been the case, they would have been unable to survive for that long. Warlike activities are said to have begun only ten thousand years ago, along with the transition, in the Neolithic period, from gathering and hunting to farming.

Since there are no warlike phenomena in nature—and, until a relatively short time ago, there were none in our history—we are not genetically programmed to withstand mistreatment as children. Animals kill their young if they don't want to care for them, but they don't torture them for years. For millions of years in the course of evolution, we have been programmed to offer loving care and protection to our newborn infants, and nature has equipped our young to receive only positive treatment. We do not have a natural mechanism for coping with mistreatment, nor can we erase it from our bodies, as everything that takes place in our lives remains registered in our cells as information. Nature gives us only the ability to anesthetize ourselves when the mistreatment becomes unbearable. Our organism protects itself against the threat of death with the help of repression and denial. We forget the beatings and the disdain, or else we maintain that they did us some good—and go on to engage in the same practices with our children. The protective mechanism used by the child thus becomes fateful for the adult and for our species, for repression leads—out of pure ignorance—to the destruction of our own children and our fellow human beings and to the acceptance of abuse as a normal way of life. It is the dangerous inattention to the childhood truth stored in our cells that makes us act destructively even though we do not really want to do so.

During the early 1980s, a number of nurses working in psychiatric clinics wrote me that reading my books helped them in their work with their patients but that they had to hide this fact from their superiors for fear of losing their jobs. Child abuse was at that time still a taboo subject in psychiatry, even though so many patients had an appalling story to tell. No one wanted to hear it—psychiatrists least of all.

In recent years, numerous books on the subject of child abuse have become available, and numerous concepts have been developed toward healing the consequences of childhood trauma. At last, even the psychiatric establishment has had to recognize that child abuse and its consequences do, indeed, exist. Sadly, however, the old blinders have been kept on, defenses against the whole truth remain almost intact, statistics and classifications are bandied about—anything to deny the fact that *all* patients suffer from the results of injuries to their psychic integrity during childhood.

In the United States, for instance, it was known in the 1970s that many Holocaust survivors—and, later, Vietnam veterans—were continuing to suffer from psychic aftereffects of the traumatic experiences they had repressed years before. This phenomenon was labeled Post-Traumatic Stress Syndrome. When the facts about child abuse became better known in the eighties, a link was made between these patients and adult survivors of child abuse; then, in the early nineties, all these people were deemed to be suffering from "Complex Post-Traumatic Stress Disorder." They were lumped together in a way that suggested, first, that people who manifested long-range damage from childhood mistreatment were rare, and, second, that their experience was essentially the same as that of people who suffered severe trauma as adults. This association is misleading in two ways: It sidesteps the fact that childhood mistreatment is the primary cause of *every* kind of psychic disorder, and it implies that the same therapeutic methods can be applied to all trauma victims, regardless of the age at which the injury was sustained.

Even when the number of patients who reported having been mistreated as children turned out to be very high—much to the surprise of psychiatrists, who until recently had denied such a possibility—it did not occur to members of the psychiatric profession to look for a new and more far-reaching system of therapy. Such patients were placed in groups and treated in accordance with the principles used for patients suffering from post-traumatic disturbances, in the belief that empowerment by the group and the chance to recount the trauma in detail would be sufficient to free them from its consequences. Apart from the fact that only a small percentage of people can remember and articulate early childhood traumas, such therapeutic methods inevitably prove illusory for all trauma sufferers, except perhaps in the case of essentially stable people who have experienced an isolated trauma in their adult years. The reason such groups are ineffective is that they ignore the specific damage done to the child's whole growing system, especially to his ability to feel and remember. Without having conscious, personal experience of this damage, psychiatrists and other mental health professionals tend to see all trauma survivors as one special category of human being and to look for a method to treat "them" and their sickness.

Some recent movements in the United States have divorced treatment from psychiatry and its limitations. Because of their moralistic and religious leanings, however, which disregard natural laws, they can offer little real help. The so-called recovery movement, for instance, is based on techniques borrowed from Transactional Analysis and Neurolinguistic Programming—the latter of which is more or less an attempt to unlearn ingrained patterns of behavior via manipulatory exercises, ignoring the emotional information these patterns have to offer us. The recovery movement is also infused with spiritual and religious concepts, such as forgiveness and a Higher Power, that seem to be necessary because, ultimately, the techniques offered are of no use and *can* be of no use. But whether a Higher Power helps in individual cases depends on individual belief, and in that sense what is offered is, at best, old wine in new bottles. Consequently, this movement does not lead to personal freedom and autonomy but rather to group-dependency and conformity, as evidenced by the similarity in the vast literature on the subject of recovery. I think that religious concepts become necessary when real procedures for self-help are lacking, either because they are unknown or just feared precisely because of their effectiveness, radical nature, and revolutionary power.

I am constantly approached by readers with doubts and queries about various "new therapies." My own reading has led me to the conclusion that with the crucial exception of Stettbacher's method, most of these "new" concepts are essentially recycled old intellectual theories. What they offer are techniques of mental and physical manipulation of one's feelings and one's true history. They also continue to move within the framework of traditional morality that protects parents at any cost. These characteristics are clearly evidenced in the Alcoholics Anonymous Twelve-Step Program, which has become a model for many others. In all of these "therapies," flight from the concrete facts of one's own personal history is—despite all assurances to the contrary—an integral part of the program. This flight from the facts is further disguised and mystified by a shared "spiritual" vocabulary.

Thus the proponents of the recovery movement offer little

help when it comes to repressed childhood feeling and memory. Indeed, they circumvent its emergence with abstraction, preferring, for example, to talk about the "dysfunctional family" rather than confront specific instances of abuse by parents. This is probably because they still fear their own parents, without knowing that they fear them, or why. If they have never themselves experienced the terror of the defenseless child they once were, then why should they be convinced it even exists? This avoidance and denial can be seen in their fidelity to traditional morality, something that any effective therapy could, and should, be able to do without. The indictment of the parents by the child—the victim—cannot be bypassed if the full impact of one's childhood injuries is to be felt. Equally crucial is the retrospective condemnation by our adult selves of the abuse perpetrated by our parents. Only then can we ensure that the victim does not one day become the perpetrator, repeating the cycle of abuse with his or her own children.

A well-known musician, for instance, can assure an interviewer that he has forgiven his father for his brutal upbringing, because in spite of it—or maybe even because of it—he has become successful. The interviewer is delighted with the musician's admirable moral position. His fans are delighted, too, and his record business goes well. But all this success, even in combination with religion, doesn't help him overcome his childhood fears. Otherwise he would not be compelled in his shows to repeat unconsciously the traumas of his childhood; most of his gestures and body stances on stage seem to depict scenes in which a child is being frightened by sexual molestation and violence. The musician seems to be trying unsuccessfully to discharge his fear, using music and body language to display what were quite possibly the actions of a molesting father. But as long as he insists on denying and not feeling the truth, this effort must be undertaken repeatedly. Alternatively, he may find a child to whom he will do what has been done to him, perhaps in a less brutal manner, and will label this behavior "love," as his father once did. As long as he believes that his father did him no harm, he is likely to remain in danger of repeating his father's deeds.

Therapies that purport to work on feelings have become fashionable today, in contrast to the more intellectually oriented schools of Freud, Jung, and Adler. As far as I can see, however, this "work" has as its primary goal not the experience and recognition of reality but a short-term emotional discharge. It is, of course, a relief to release powerful feelings. But as long as that release is not accompanied by a recognition of the true situation, which makes the intensity of the feelings both comprehensible and legitimate, and as long as the truth is avoided, as is the practice in many programs that preach forgiveness, then the old, self-destructive patterns of behavior cannot be resolved.

The same applies to so-called body work. The artificial reawakening of the physical memory of traumatic situations by means of special breathing techniques or massage cannot bring lasting resolution of the effects of such traumas, although it may bring short-term relief. The reawakening of traumas exclusively at the physical level is useless, and often dangerous, if they are not integrated into one's entire life history. Only then can bodily sensations be understood and resolved. If we do not work on all three levels—body, feeling, mind—the symptoms of our distress will keep returning, as the body goes on repeating the story stored in its cells until it is finally listened to and understood.

Therapy brings permanent benefits only when the *truth* about *the past* is made accessible and remains accessible for the rest of our lives. Only if we remain open to our constantly evolving feelings—today, tomorrow, the day after tomorrow— and have the tools to understand them can we claim health, clarity, and independence for ourselves. Claim them, and maintain them. Only thus can we keep our feet on firm ground, and not be dependent on drugs, gurus, groups, or theories that teach us how to change our past.

An extreme example will illustrate just how dangerous the consequences of the denial of the past can be. The *New York Times* reported (July 11, 1993) that over the last five years neo-Nazi groups in America, with the help of a number of teachers, have succeeded in casting doubt on the reality of the Holocaust. As many as 22 percent of the schoolchildren interviewed believed that eyewitness accounts of the Holocaust were lies. And this is in America, where there is not even the burden of guilt that exists in Germany. The reality of the events in Europe from 1940 to 1945 is, of course, so terrifying that today's children can be forgiven for wanting to deny it; an unscrupulous teacher would have to do little to strengthen their doubts. But such a rewriting of history will inevitably have horrendous consequences in the future, as people are forced to learn once again, from the deaths of more millions of people, what they could have learned from the past.

In a similar way, Freud did not want to believe that parents ever torture their children, even though his own discoveries clearly proved that some parents do. But relativizing, glossing over, or distorting a terrible reality can lead neither to individual healing nor to successful resolution of political problems. It can succeed only in deepening darkness, perpetuating ignorance, and aggravating the symptoms of our ills, both social and individual.

Many writers try to escape the pain of their own childhood by preaching forgiveness, discipline, goodwill, and "spirituality" to themselves and others, as though these practices could extinguish the truth stored in the body. But the body can't be deceived; it knows our true story very precisely. Intellectual generalizations cannot help us gain access to the secrets with which we have unconsciously lived for decades. Those secrets have first to be articulated via our feelings, because as infants who had to repress our pain and helpless rage, we were *incapable of thinking: we could only feel.* Using hypnosis to recall memories, without consciously experiencing the strong emotions and without understanding the justified outrage of the child we were, is thus of no help either.

Other approaches focus on simply discharging feelings in order to be rid of them. If we don't have the courage to face the feelings we have repressed, however, they will continue to block our development and threaten our physical health. We must experience them, integrate them in the context of our whole life history, and remain open to the emergence of new feelings; otherwise we will continue to be shut off from the information they have to give us. As children, we had no choice but to learn the skills of repression in order to survive. As adults, we can—and must—welcome and assist in the breakdown of that repression if we want to live our lives more freely and meaningfully and avoid subjecting our own children to what we repressed long ago but still carry in ourselves.

Readers of *Drama* sometimes write to me describing actual physical reactions they have had while reading the book. I find these accounts encouraging, because they indicate that these people have not been sidetracked into intellectualizing; instead, the very process of reading the book has made their experience accessible, so that they can begin to find out what actually happened to them. One reader described how he had a sudden attack of stomach cramps while reading a particular passage and threw the book down in a rage. Only when an outburst of tears made clear to him the connection between his stomach cramps and the passage he had been reading, and when he allowed himself to experience the attendant feelings, did his cramps disappear. He could then pick up the book again.

Some physician authors who have worked with people suffering from life-threatening illnesses have tried to help them get well by talking to them about their "emotional problems." This so-called love medicine does in some cases appear to provide temporary relief. I can imagine that it would bring a measure of hope to a cancer patient, for example, to hear for the first time that her illness has something to do with her soul, with her thoughts and feelings. But just to tell a person that her emotional life is involved in her cancer is not enough. If she is not encouraged and helped to discover her own, specific history, if she does not learn to feel a full range of emotions and to give up her illusions and self-betrayal, discussing her emotions cannot help the process of healing. Hope will most likely either vanish or become a useless shield against recognizing the progress of the disease.

What very ill patients usually hear are calls for forgiveness, affirmations, and meditations. They are told to have "positive thoughts" and to be loving and brave—all the traditional demands that the child once placed upon herself in order to protect her parents by concealing their abuse and that have brought on her illness. If we are not allowed to feel and express what happened to us, our lives become senseless. Most cancer patients live—and die—upholding an idealized image against the painful truth of their past. They are proud of being resolute and altruistic, not demanding anything for themselves. It is only their illness that strives to express the almost extinguished hope of being listened to and understood. Nobody wants to know that history, however; it might remind the doctors, the nurses, and the hospice volunteers of their own painful, buried past. The patient herself is unaware of how hungry she is, how she is longing not only for affection but also for the truth; and she doesn't realize that she herself is the only person who can redeem her from her plight, from her dangerous self-denial.

Doctors would be able to help many more people regain health if they were better informed, if they knew that a person can recover even from serious illness if he is ready to live with his past instead of dying in opposition to it—and if he has the tools to begin to do so. I know of a man who had been brought up in an atmosphere of constant terror mingled with hypocrisy, yet he was too afraid and too deeply indoctrinated with moralistic and religious ideas to allow himself to feel the desperate rage this mistreatment had left buried within him. Although his parents had died several years earlier, he was still so frightened of them that the only way he could express his unspoken, unconscious rage was to turn it against himself and develop lung cancer. As his parents had done before, he was unconsciously rejecting himself and his life, although consciously he did everything he could to recover, including adhering to a raw-food diet. The regimen he followed brought him a total recovery from the cancer. Unfortunately, however, the weight of his unconscious despair was stronger than his conscious wish to heal. He gave up the diet very soon after his recovery, even though he believed it had helped him almost miraculously, and developed another kind of cancer, which eventually caused his death.

This example is not intended to indicate that raw food is useless in fighting cancer, but is instead meant to show that in order to decisively counteract a life-threatening disease, with whatever means, you must be determined to save your life— the only one you have—because you really *want* to live it, on the unconscious as well as the conscious level. To feel your legitimate rage is, in fact, a powerful and effective weapon. It is not destructive; feelings that are not repressed, that are instead consciously experienced, never kill anyone.

In fact, most illnesses are nothing other than a language permitted the abused child, as represented by the adult body. How else is the truth of a tormented, unwanted, and betrayed child to find an outlet in our society? Unfortunately, however, it still seems forbidden to understand this language. Scientists work diligently on the immune system in the hope of finding a way to fool it once and for all and in so doing keep the inner truth of the patient hidden forever.

However, an illness can be a signal, an alarm, a way of reminding us of a very early state of distress. If we are willing to face this distress, to look for its reasons, we don't need the indirect language of the immune system and we can be cured, also without medication. The medical/health authorities will hardly support us on this path, because they are yet unaware of its existence.

The drug addict takes the risk of becoming a criminal and socially discriminated only to avoid facing the truth stored up in his own body. He tries again and again to deceive his cells with increasing amounts of these substances. Because society as a whole, including most professionals, ignores or denies the reality of his suffering, he will be confronted with "solutions" that pretend to help him but don't provide any real help. Some professionals maintain that free access to heroin can reduce crime, and that the oral use of methadone, a drug substitute, can diminish the risk of AIDS because contamination by a dirty needle can then be more easily avoided. Even if these assumptions turned out to be true, the crucial problem of the addict (the physical drive to numb oneself) and the actual causes of this plight are totally overlooked in such considerations.

Every kind of addiction is a way of escaping from the memories of one's own painful life history. And every addict can overcome the addiction if she or he is really ready to confront their memories. The manipulative resources of the health care system do not help. As long as a person prefers to live in constant misery rather than face his own history, nobody can help him. But as long as someone remains uninformed of the other options available, we cannot know what she *might* be able to do once society stops encouraging her blindness. It is not just the will to free oneself from addiction that can really liberate a person, as is maintained by Alcoholics Anonymous; it is the will and the determination to find and resolve the *causes* of one's addiction, which always lay hidden in childhood.

Society offers us a rich palette of respectable alternatives to letting ourselves feel or recognize the damage our confused, and confusing, parents did to us—the havoc they wrought in our developing and highly fragile organisms. With the help of the genetic theory or sophisticated speculation, we can try to evade these simple but painful facts. For example, we can refute the idea of causality as an old-fashioned, mechanistic way of thinking and dress up our denial in a "new," "scientific" paradigm for the postmodern world, based on the "philosophy" of the Twelve-Step Program. Or we can keep our memories at bay by declaring war on logic and becoming devotees of the irrational. We can abandon the individual self (that is, abandon our own feelings and history) and strive to attain Nirvana or merge with "The Whole" as we sit in meditation. We can write volumes of prose and thereby confuse more millions of people. We can travel the world using the authority conferred upon us to prevent the faithful from practicing birth control, so that even more unwanted children will be born, children who will later be neglected and abused. We can mobilize whole nations to fight against one another; we can wage wars and raise the flag of victory. And why not? To confuse others is, after all, easier—far easier—than to feel the terrible confusion of the helpless child we once were. Flight from the past is our way of life, and millions gratefully accept its rewards. Given the choice, who of us wouldn't prefer to go on fleeing from our history? But for some, flight no longer functions. Some people want to find out who they are and how they became what they are.

The consequences of such flights from reality have barely begun to be investigated. Fortunately, however, the laboratories, which receive no research grants from the state, are to be found in each and every one of us. Our courage and daring in facing the prosaic facts of our personal history, in which we have previously been blindly enmeshed, will ultimately endow us with the understanding we need. Once we can see the truth for ourselves, we will no longer be misled by pseudo-knowledge.

In the years since the original *Drama* was written, I have come to understand many things that I either did not see at the time or, as I must concede today, covered too peripherally. I would like to summarize some of those points here, as well as to refer those who wish to find out more about these themes to my later works:

1. Earlier in my life I tried very hard to understand and make clear to others the motivation of parents who injure their children. As a result, I gave the impression that the effort to understand the parents' point of view should be part of any therapy. The opposite is in fact true. If we attempt to understand the feelings of those who injured us, we will lose contact with our own feelings, the very feelings that are crucial to recognizing our injuries and healing them. Feeling our own pain, and not that of our parents, is essential to the successful outcome of any therapy. Without a clear perspective on this (a perspective that was lacking in the original version of the *Drama*), we cannot help ourselves. Nor can we help our parents. But they can help themselves, if they are willing and ready to feel

and resolve their plight on their own and not at the cost of their children.

2. My own experience has taught me that the enactment of *forgiveness*—which, sixteen years ago, I still believed to be right—brings the therapeutic process to a halt. It *blocks* the unfolding of feelings and perceptions that are impossible to experience at the early stages of therapy, but that, with an increase in inner strength and resilience, can eventually be faced. Some memories surface years after the beginning of self-therapy, when we have finally become strong enough to face them. This fruitful surfacing of new memories must not be hindered by the closure that forgiveness would produce (see Miller, 1993).

3. Simply talking about our feelings is useless and gets us nowhere, yet many people spend years in traditional therapy doing just that, without undergoing the slightest change. The fact that they don't even realize this is happening makes the situation even more tragic. To gain access to our own truth, we must experience and articulate our feelings in the context of the inner dialogue. For those who seriously want to remedy the consequences of childhood traumatization, all traditional methods are useless, misleading, and potentially dangerous, for they strengthen our intellectual defenses against feeling and prevent the disclosure of repressed memories, even when the therapist or analyst encourages the patient to "talk about the trauma" of being abused, sexually or otherwise.

In intellectual therapies, suspicions, assumptions, or suggestions given by therapists cannot be checked for accuracy or confirmed. They may be right or wrong, but even if they are right, the knowledge will be ineffective in the patient's search for healing. Only our feelings and body sensations, of which we become aware during the loudly spoken inner dialogue, can make us certain of what really happened to us. Only with *their* answers can we retrieve repressed memories and integrate the knowledge so won, although reliable information from family members can provide additional confirmation. In some misguided therapies, people can come to false or uncertain conclusions on the basis of intellectual processes, but these conclusions are not memories. The term "false memory" is misleading and, in fact, self-contradictory (see Miller 1990a).

4. "New" methods that claim to work with "feelings" but actually employ traditional morality and ideology prevent us from seeing our reality. The most they can offer is short-term relief. If the therapeutic process stops short of the integration of the whole truth, then we will continue to be dependent on groups and "Higher Powers." After the initial feeling of euphoria, the return of depression can be held at bay by devoting oneself to winning over new converts, but these new converts will, in turn, need potential followers. This, incidentally, seems the most likely explanation for the exponential increase in devotees, irrespective of the weakness of the ideas (see Miller 1993).

5. It is a great mistake to imagine that one can resolve traumas in a symbolic fashion. If that were possible, poets, painters, and other artists would be able to resolve their pain through creativity. This is not the case, however. Creativity helps us channel the pain of trauma into symbolic acts; it doesn't help us resolve it. If symbolic revenge for maltreatment received in childhood were effective, then dictators would eventually stop humiliating and torturing their fellow human beings. As long as they choose to deceive themselves about who really deserves their hatred, however, and as long as they go on feeding that hatred in symbolic form instead of experiencing and resolving it within the context of their own childhood, their hunger for revenge will remain insatiable (see Miller 1990a).

6. The mistreatment of children is not the inevitable fate of humankind, as I believed at the time the *Drama* was written. It

can be prevented by repairing the damage done in our own childhood, through practicing the self-therapy. Parents who have confronted the pain of their past will not mistreat their children.

7. The prevention of child abuse is possible with greater public awareness. Much unnecessary suffering could be prevented if, for example, recent discoveries about the importance of *bonding* between a mother and her newborn child (through eye and body contact) were more widely disseminated. Bonding gives the child greater security and safety for its later life by triggering in the mother a hormonal release that takes place only at that time and only in the presence of the newborn and that better establishes her love for the child. A woman who has bonded with her child in the first moments of becoming a mother will be in less danger of mistreating him and will be better able to protect him from both her own past and that of his father. The experience of her love for the child and the child's love for and helpless dependence on her can help motivate her to resolve her repressed pain. If she does not do so, the destructive power of her unconscious can still continue to operate and to harm the child.

8. I am often asked why some people who were abused as children do not in turn abuse their own children. I have addressed this question in my books *Banished Knowledge* and *Breaking Down the Wall of Silence,* where I have tried to explain the crucial role of the "helping witness" in childhood and the "enlightened witness" in adulthood. I do not know of anyone, however, who, having been abused in childhood, did not then behave in a destructive (or at least a self-destructive) way in adulthood, as long as she continued to deny the abuse she had to endure.

9. I have often been confronted by readers and therapists with the problems created for survivors of abuse by propo-

nents of the so-called False Memory Syndrome and by the activities of groups that support "falsely accused" parents in their attempts to suppress the reports of their adult children. I think these efforts on the part of parents, authorities, and lawyers are motivated not only by the desire to defend their innocence and by financial self-interest but also, and above all, by a much deeper reason: the fear of their own repressed history. The reports of survivors who have discovered the truth after a long period of denial or dissociation are seen as a threat both because they blame and accuse and because they trigger the past in others. They present a challenge to the power of repression. Parents, judges, and attorneys may ask themselves, consciously or unconsciously, "If this is true, if such terrible things happened to Ann and to Mary, and they didn't know it for decades, then how can I be certain that I am not hiding a similar story inside myself?" Only by believing that these things did not happen, by believing instead in the "false memory" theory, can they continue to live as they did before.

10.   Finally, I would like to make it clear that the term "the inner child," which is frequently ascribed to me, does not in fact originate with me but was taken from Transactional Analysis. I regard the term as misleading and consequently have employed this metaphor *only* in a very particular context. Specifically, I spoke of the "child within me" when I described the importance of painting in my life in a book that incorporated some of my pictures (see Miller 1986 and 1995). I will cite the relevant passage here:

> The child within me . . . appeared . . . late in life, wanting to tell me her secret.
> She approached very hesitantly, speaking to me in an inarticulate way, but she took me by the hand and led me into territory I had been avoiding all my life because it frightened me. Yet I had

to go there; I could not keep on turning my back, for it was my territory, my very own. It was the place I had attempted to forget so many years ago, the same place where I had abandoned the child I once was. There she had to stay, alone with her knowledge, waiting until someone would come at last to listen to her and believe her. Now I was standing at an open door, ill-prepared, filled with an adult's fear of the darkness and menace of the past, but I could not bring myself to close the door and leave the child alone again until my death. Instead, I made a decision that was to change my life profoundly: to let the child lead me, to put my trust in this nearly autistic being who had survived the isolation of decades.

*We are all prisoners of our childhood, whether we know it, suspect it, deny it, or have never even heard about the possibility.* The realization that we can free ourselves from the consequences of old wounds will gain ground as more people prove it can be done. Inevitably, resistance to following this path is great, as we all fear our repressed past and the experience of how helpless we once were. We have had good reason to be afraid; if we did not, there would have been no need for repression. Yet the more we encounter our fear and dare to face its causes, the more it decreases.

I have no doubt that one day, thanks to J. Konrad Stettbacher's new therapeutic method, all attempts to evade the truth by means of ideology will cease to have a purpose. They will be unnecessary, as soon as the truth is accessible to every one of us. Stettbacher's therapeutic concept works because it is based on the laws of nature and does not take refuge in religious and moralistic beliefs that ignore these laws. Men and women have the ability to process their experience, if their integrity has not been damaged. Thanks to his Four-Step Method, Stettbacher has managed to help even those with the severest psychic injuries recover that ability.

If they make use of this method, people can one day come to

realize, among other things, that nationalism was a means of legitimizing their hatred. They will realize that although this hatred had very real and terrible causes, it actually had nothing to do with countries, flags, songs, or wars. They will see its real source in the cruelty with which they grew up. They will no longer find it necessary to persecute and destroy other nations in an effort to regain the self-confidence that was once annihilated in them. They will realize their true needs—what they rightfully long for, the needs that are our birthright. They will allow themselves neither to be consoled by vague promises of eternity nor to be talked out of their rightful needs. Instead, they will want to reclaim their lives and create in the here-and-now that which they so tragically missed in their own childhood: truthfulness, clarity, and respect for themselves and others.

ALICE MILLER
1994

*Translated by Simon Worrall*

# 1

# The Drama of the Gifted Child and How We Became Psychotherapists

EXPERIENCE has taught us that we have only one enduring weapon in our struggle against mental illness: the emotional discovery of the truth about the unique history of our childhood. Is it possible, then, to free ourselves altogether from illusions? History demonstrates that they sneak in everywhere, that every life is full of them—perhaps because the truth often seems unbearable to us. And yet the truth is so essential that its loss exacts a heavy toll, in the form of grave illness. In order to become whole we must try, in a long process, to discover our own personal truth, a truth that may cause pain before giving us a new sphere of freedom. If we choose instead to content ourselves with intellectual "wisdom," we will remain in the sphere of illusion and self-deception.

The damage done to us during our childhood cannot be undone, since we cannot change anything in our past. We can, however, change ourselves. We can repair ourselves and gain our lost integrity by choosing to look more closely at the knowledge that is stored inside our bodies and bringing this knowledge closer to our awareness. This path, although certainly not easy, is the only route by which we can at last leave behind the cruel, invisible prison of our childhood. We become free by transforming ourselves from unaware victims of the past into responsible individuals in the present, who are aware of our past and are thus able to live with it.

Most people do exactly the opposite. Without realizing that the past is constantly determining their present actions, they avoid learning anything about their history. They continue to live in their repressed childhood situation, ignoring the fact that it no longer exists. They are continuing to fear and avoid dangers that, although once real, have not been real for a long time. They are driven by unconscious memories and by repressed feelings and needs that, in a perverse manner, determine nearly everything they do or fail to do.

The repression of brutal abuse experienced during childhood drives many people to destroy their lives and the lives of others. In an unconscious thirst for revenge, they may engage in acts of violence, burning homes and businesses and physically attacking other people, using this destruction to hide the truth from themselves and avoid feeling the despair of the tormented child they once were. Such acts are often done in the name of "patriotism" or religious beliefs.

Other people actively continue the torture once inflicted upon them in self-scourging clubs of every sort and in sadomasochistic practices. They think of such activities as "liberation." Women who allow their nipples to be pierced in order to hang rings from them can then pose for newspaper photographs, proudly saying that they felt no pain when having it done and that it was even fun for them. One need not doubt the truth of their statements; they had to learn very early in life not to feel pain, and today they would go to any lengths not to feel the pain of the little girl who was once sexually exploited by her father and had to imagine that it was fun for her.

Repressed pain may reveal itself more privately, as in a woman, sexually exploited as a child, who has denied her childhood reality and in order not to feel the pain is perpetually fleeing her past with the help of men, alcohol, drugs, or achievement. She needs a constant thrill to keep boredom at bay; not even one moment of quiet can be permitted during which the burning loneliness of her childhood experience might be felt, for she fears that feeling more than death. She will continue in her flight unless she learns that the awareness of old feelings is not deadly but liberating. What often *does* kill is the rejection of those feelings, the conscious experience of which could reveal the truth.

The repression of childhood pain influences not only the life of an individual but also the taboos of the whole society. The usual run of biographies illustrates this very clearly. In reading the biographies of famous artists, for example, one gains the impression that their lives began at puberty. Before that, we are told, they had a "happy," "contented," or "untroubled" childhood, or one that was "full of deprivation" or "very stimulating." But what a particular childhood really was like does not seem to interest these biographers—as if the roots of a whole life were not hidden and entwined in its childhood. I should like to illustrate this with a simple example.

Henry Moore describes in his memoirs how, as a small boy, he massaged his mother's back with an oil to soothe her rheumatism. Reading this suddenly threw light for me on Moore's sculptures: the great, reclining women with the tiny heads—I could now see in them the mother through the small boy's eyes, with the head high above, in diminishing perspective, and the back close before him and enormously enlarged. This interpretation may be irrelevant for many art critics, but for me it demonstrates how strongly a child's experiences may endure in his unconscious and what possibilities of expression they may awaken in the adult who is free to give them rein. Now, Moore's memory did not concern a traumatic event and so could survive intact. But every childhood's traumatic experiences remain hidden and locked in darkness, and the key to our understanding of the life that follows is hidden away with them.

## THE POOR RICH CHILD

I sometimes ask myself whether it will ever be possible for us to grasp the extent of the loneliness and desertion to which we were exposed as children.* Here I do not mean to speak, primarily, of children who were obviously uncared for or totally neglected, and who were always aware of this or at least grew up with the knowledge that it was so. Apart from these extreme cases, there are large numbers of people who enter therapy in the belief (with which they grew up) that their childhood was happy and protected.

Quite often I have been faced with people who were praised and admired for their talents and their achievements, who were toilet-trained in the first year of their lives, and who may even, at the age of one and a half to five, have capably helped to take care of their younger siblings. According to prevailing attitudes, these people—the pride of their parents—should have had a strong and stable sense of self-assurance. But the case is exactly the opposite. They do well, even excellently, in everything they undertake; they are admired and envied; they are successful whenever they care to be—but behind all this lurks depression, a feeling of emptiness and self-alienation, and a sense that their life has no meaning. These dark feelings will

*Today, in 1994, I know that this is, in principle, possible.

come to the fore as soon as the drug of grandiosity fails, as soon as they are not "on top," not definitely the "superstar," or whenever they suddenly get the feeling they have failed to live up to some ideal image or have not measured up to some standard. Then they are plagued by anxiety or deep feelings of guilt and shame. What are the reasons for such disturbances in these competent, accomplished people?

In the very first interview they will let the listener know that they have had understanding parents, or at least one such, and if they are aware of having been misunderstood as children, they feel that the fault lay with them and with their inability to express themselves appropriately. They recount their earliest memories without any sympathy for the child they once were, and this is the more striking as these patients not only have a pronounced introspective ability but seem, to some degree, to be able to empathize with other people. Their access to the emotional world of their own childhood, however, is impaired—characterized by a lack of respect, a compulsion to control and manipulate, and a demand for achievement. Very often they show disdain and irony, even derision and cynicism, for the child they were. In general, there is a complete absence of real emotional understanding or serious appreciation of their own childhood vicissitudes, and no conception of their true needs—beyond the desire for achievement. The repression of their real history has been so complete that their illusion of a good childhood can be maintained with ease.

As a basis for a description of the psychic climate of these persons, some general assumptions should be made clear:

- The child has a primary need from the very beginning of her life to be regarded and respected as the person she really is at any given time.

- When we speak here of "the person she really is at any given time," we mean emotions, sensations, and their expression from the first day onward.

- In an atmosphere of respect and tolerance for her feelings, the child, in the phase of separation, will be able to give up symbiosis with the mother and accomplish the steps toward individuation and autonomy.

- If they are to furnish these prerequisites for the healthy development of their child, the parents themselves ought to have grown up in such an atmosphere. If they did, they will be able to assure the child the protection and well-being she needs to develop trust.

- Parents who did not experience this climate as children are themselves deprived; throughout their lives they will continue to look for what their own parents could not give them at the appropriate time—the presence of a person who is completely aware of them and takes them seriously.

- This search, of course, can never fully succeed, since it relates to a situation that belongs irrevocably to the past, namely to the time right after birth and during early childhood.

- A person with this unsatisfied and unconscious (because repressed) need will nevertheless be compelled to attempt its gratification through substitute means, as long as she ignores her repressed life history.

- The most efficacious objects for substitute gratification are a parent's *own children.* The newborn baby or small child is completely dependent on his parents, and since their caring is essential for his existence, he does all he can to avoid losing them. From the very first day onward, he will muster all his resources to this end, like a small plant that turns toward the sun in order to survive.

In my work with people in the helping professions, I have often been confronted with a childhood history that seems significant to me.

- There was a *mother** who at the core was emotionally insecure and who depended for her equilibrium on her child's behaving in a particular way. This mother was able to hide her insecurity from her child and from everyone else behind a hard, authoritarian, even totalitarian facade.
- This child had an amazing ability to perceive and respond intuitively, that is, unconsciously, to this need of the mother, or of both parents, for him to take on the role that had unconsciously been assigned to him.
- This role secured "love" for the child—that is, his parents' exploitation. He could sense that he was needed, and this need guaranteed him a measure of existential security.

This ability is then extended and perfected. Later, these children not only become mothers (confidantes, comforters, advisers, supporters) of their own mothers but also take over at least part of the responsibility for their siblings and eventually develop a special sensitivity to unconscious signals manifesting the needs of others. No wonder they often choose to become psychotherapists later on. Who else, without this previous history, would muster sufficient interest to spend the whole day trying to discover what is happening in other people's unconscious? But the development and perfecting of this sensitivity—which once assisted the child in surviving and now

*By "mother" I here refer to the person closest to the child during the first years of life. This need not be the biological mother, or even a woman. In the course of the past twenty years, many fathers have assumed this mothering function (Mütterlichkeit).

enables the adult to pursue his strange profession—also contain the roots of his emotional disturbance: As long as the therapist is not aware of his repression, it can compel him to use his patients, who depend on him, to meet his unmet needs with substitutes.

## THE LOST WORLD OF FEELINGS

On the basis of my experience, I think that the cause of an emotional disturbance is to be found in the infant's early adaptation. The child's needs for respect, echoing, understanding, sympathy, and mirroring have had to be repressed, with several serious consequences.

One such consequence is the person's inability to experience consciously certain feelings of his own (such as jealousy, envy, anger, loneliness, helplessness, or anxiety), either in childhood or later in adulthood. This is all the more tragic in that we are concerned here with lively people who are often capable of deep feelings. It is most noticeable when they describe childhood experiences that were free of pain and fear. They could enjoy their encounters with nature, for example, without hurting the mother or making her feel insecure, reducing her power, or endangering her equilibrium. It is remarkable how these attentive, lively, and sensitive children, who can, for example, remember exactly how they discovered the sunlight in bright grass at the age of four, at eight were unable to "notice anything" or show any curiosity about their pregnant mother, or were "not at all" jealous at the birth of a sibling. It is also remarkable how, at the age of two, such a child could be left alone and "be good" while soldiers forced their way into the house and searched it, suffering the terrifying intrusion quietly and without crying. These people have all developed the art of not experiencing feelings, for a child can experience her feelings only when there is somebody there who accepts her fully, understands her, and supports her. If that person is missing, if the child must risk losing the mother's love or the love of her substitute in order to feel, then she will repress her emotions. She cannot even experience them secretly, "just for herself"; she will fail to experience them at all. But they will nevertheless stay in her body, in her cells, stored up as information that can be triggered by a later event.

Throughout their later life, these people will have to deal with situations in which these rudimentary feelings may awaken, but without the original connection ever becoming clear. The connection can be deciphered only when the intense emotions have been experienced in therapy and successfully linked with their original situation.[*]

Take, for example, the feeling of abandonment—not that of the adult, who feels lonely and therefore turns to alcohol or drugs, goes to the movies, visits friends, or makes "unnecessary" telephone calls in order to bridge the gap somehow. No, I mean the original feeling in the small infant, who had none of these means of distraction and whose communication, verbal or preverbal, did not reach the mother because his mother herself was deprived. For her part, she was dependent on a specific echo from the child that was essential to her, for she herself was a child in search of a person who could be available to her.

However paradoxical this may seem, a child is at the mother's disposal. The mother can feel herself the center of attention, for her child's eyes follow her everywhere. A child cannot run away from her as her own mother once did. A child can be brought up so that it becomes what she wants it to be. A child

---

[*]In the therapy method developed by J. K. Stettbacher, this phenomenon plays an essential role.

can be made to show respect; she can impose her own feelings on him, see herself mirrored in his love and admiration, and feel strong in his presence. But when he becomes too much, she can abandon that child to a stranger or to solitary confinement in another room.

When a woman has had to repress all these needs in relation to her own mother, they will arise from the depth of her unconscious and seek gratification through her own child, however well-educated she may be. The child feels this clearly and very soon forgoes the expression of his own distress. Later, when these feelings of being deserted begin to emerge in the therapy of the adult, they are accompanied by intense pain and despair. It is clear that these people could not have survived so much pain as children. That would have been possible only in an empathic, attentive environment, which was lacking. Thus all feelings had to be warded off. But to say that they were *absent* would be a denial of the empirical evidence.

Several mechanisms can be recognized in the defense against early feelings of abandonment. In addition to simple denial, we usually find the exhausting struggle to fulfill the old, repressed, and by now often perverted needs with the help of symbols (cults, sexual perversions, groups of all kinds, alcohol, or drugs). Intellectualization is very commonly encountered as well, since it is a defense mechanism of great power. It can have disastrous results, however, when the mind ignores the vital messages of the body (see my reflections on Nietzsche's illness in *The Untouched Key* [1990] and *Breaking Down the Wall of Silence* [1991]). All these defense mechanisms are accompanied by repression of the original situation and the emotions belonging to it.

Accommodation to parental needs often (but not always) leads to the "as-if personality." This person develops in such a way that he reveals only what is expected of him and fuses so completely with what he reveals that one could scarcely guess how much more there is to him behind this false self. He cannot develop and differentiate his true self, because he is unable to live it. Understandably, this person will complain of a sense of emptiness, futility, or homelessness, for the emptiness is real. A process of emptying, impoverishment, and crippling of his potential actually took place. The integrity of the child was injured when all that was alive and spontaneous in him was cut off. In childhood, these patients have often had dreams in which they experienced themselves as at least partly dead. A young woman, Lisa, reported a recurrent dream:

> My younger siblings are standing on a bridge and throw a box into the river. I know that I am lying in it, dead, and yet I hear my heart beating; at this moment I always wake.

This dream combined her unconscious rage toward her younger siblings, for whom Lisa always had to be a loving, caring mother, with "killing" her own feelings, wishes, and demands. A young man, Bob, dreamed:

> I see a green meadow, on which there is a white coffin. I am afraid that my mother is in it, but I open the lid and, luckily, it is not my mother but me.

If Bob had been able as a child to express his disappointment with his mother—to experience his rage and anger—he could have stayed fully alive. But that would have led to the loss of his mother's love, and that, for a child, can mean the same as death. So he "killed" his anger, and with it a part of himself, in order to preserve the love of his mother. A young girl used to dream:

> I am lying on my bed. I am dead. My parents are talking and looking at me but they don't realize that I am dead.

The difficulties inherent in experiencing and developing one's own emotions lead to mutual dependency, which prevents individuation. Both parties have an interest in bond permanence. The parents have found in their child's false self the confirmation they were looking for, a substitute for their own missing security; the child, who has been unable to build up his own sense of security, is first consciously and then unconsciously dependent on his parents. He cannot rely on his own emotions, has not come to experience them through trial and error, has no sense of his own real needs, and is alienated from himself to the highest degree. Under these circumstances he cannot separate from his parents, and even as an adult he is still dependent on affirmation from his partner, from groups, and especially from his own children. The legacy of the parents is yet another generation condemned to hide from the true self while operating unconsciously under the influence of repressed memories. Unless the heir casts off his "inheritance" by becoming fully conscious of his true past, and thus of his true nature, loneliness in the parental home will necessarily be followed by an adulthood lived in emotional isolation.

## IN SEARCH OF THE TRUE SELF

How can therapy be of help here? It cannot give us back our lost childhood, nor can it change the past facts. No one can heal by maintaining or fostering illusion. The paradise of pre-ambivalent harmony, for which so many patients hope, is unattainable. But the experience of one's own truth, and the post-ambivalent knowledge of it, make it possible to return to one's own world of feelings at an adult level—without paradise, but with the ability to mourn. And this ability does, indeed, give us back our vitality.

It is one of the turning points in therapy when the patient comes to the emotional insight that all the love she has captured with so much effort and self-denial was not meant for her as she really was, that the admiration for her beauty and achievements was aimed at this beauty and these achievements and not at the child herself. In therapy, the small and lonely child that is hidden behind her achievements wakes up and asks: "What would have happened if I had appeared before you sad, needy, angry, furious? Where would your love have been then? And I was all these things as well. Does this mean that it was not really me you loved, but only what I pretended to be? The well-behaved, reliable, empathic, understanding, and convenient child, who in fact was never a child at all? What became of my childhood? Have I not been cheated out of it? I can never return to it. I can never make up for it. From the beginning I have been a little adult. My abilities—were they simply misused?"

These questions are accompanied by much grief and pain, but the result is always a new authority that is establishing itself in the patient—a new empathy with her own fate, born out of mourning. Now the patient does not make light of manifestations of her self any more, does not so often laugh or jeer at them, even if she still unconsciously passes them over or ignores them, in the same subtle way that her parents dealt with the child before she had any words to express her needs. Even as an older child, she was not allowed to say, or even to think: "I can be sad or happy whenever anything makes me sad or happy; I don't have to look cheerful for someone else, and I don't have to suppress my distress or anxiety to fit other people's needs. I can be angry and no one will die or get a headache because of it. I can rage when you hurt me, without losing you."

In the majority of cases, it is a great relief to a patient to see that she can now recognize and take seriously the things she used to choke off, even if the old patterns come back, again and again, over a long period. But now she begins to understand that this strategy was her only chance to survive. Now she can *realize* how she still sometimes tries to persuade herself, when she is scared, that she is not; how she belittles her feelings to protect herself, and either does not become aware of them at all, or does so only several days after they have already passed. Gradually, she realizes how she is forced to look for distraction when she is moved, upset, or sad. (When a six-year-old's mother died, his aunt told him: "You must be brave; don't cry; now go to your room and play nicely.")

Once the therapeutic process has started, it will continue if it is not interrupted by interpretations or other types of intellectual defense. The suffering person begins to be articulate and breaks with her former compliant attitudes, but because of her early experience she cannot believe she is not incurring mortal danger; she fears rejection and punishment when she defends her rights in the present. The patient is surprised by feelings she would rather not have recognized, but now it is too late: Awareness of her own impulses has already been aroused, and there is no going back.

Now the once intimidated and silenced child can experience herself in a way she had never before thought possible, and afterward she can enjoy the relief of having taken the risk and been true to herself. Whereas she had always despised miserliness, she suddenly catches herself counting up the two minutes lost to her session through a telephone call. Whereas she had previously never made demands herself and had always been tireless in fulfilling the demands of others, now she is suddenly furious that her therapist is again going on vacation. Or she is annoyed to see other people waiting outside the consulting room. What can this be? Surely not jealousy. That is an emotion she does not know! And yet: "What are they doing here? Do others besides me come here?" She hadn't realized that before.

At first it will be mortifying to see that she is not always good, understanding, tolerant, controlled, and, above all, without needs, for these have been the basis of her self-respect.

Through therapy we come to understand that we are not always as guilty as we feel, nor as innocent as we would like to believe. How can we know what kind of damage we have inflicted on others, on our children for instance, as long as our feelings are blocked, as long as we ignore our history? The confrontation with our own reality will help us give up the illusions that disguise our past, and if we then discover that we have hurt or damaged another person, we must apologize. This will make us free to resolve the old, unconscious, and unjustified feelings of guilt stemming from our childhood. We were not responsible for the cruelty inflicted on us, and yet we feel guilty. If we don't allow ourselves to recognize our wrongdoings in the present and take steps to correct them, we will not be able to resolve our unreal guilt feelings from the past.

Many people continue to pass on the cruel deeds and attitudes to which they were subjected as children, so that they can continue to idealize their parents. Psychologically, they remain small, dependent children, even in old age. They don't understand that if they had been able to admit and experience early feelings, they would feel stronger and more coherent and would become more authentic and honest with themselves and others. If we take advantage of this process, it in turn enables us to expose ourselves to emotions that well up out of earliest childhood and to experience the helplessness and ambivalence of that period.

There is a big difference between having ambivalent feelings toward someone as an adult and suddenly experiencing oneself as a two-year-old being fed by the maid in the kitchen and thinking in despair: "Why does Mom go out every evening?

Why does she not take pleasure in me? What is wrong with me that she prefers to go to other people? What can I do to make her stay home? Just don't cry, just don't cry." Peter as a two-year-old child could not have thought in these words, but in the therapeutic session where he experienced this reality, he was both an adult and a toddler, and could cry bitterly. It was not a cathartic crying, but rather the integration of his earlier longing for his mother, which until now he had always denied. In the following weeks Peter went through all the torments of his ambivalence toward his mother, who was a successful pediatrician. Her previously "frozen," idealized portrait melted into the picture of a woman who had not been able to give her child any continuity in their relationship. "I hated those beasts who were constantly sick and always taking you away from me. I hated you because you preferred being with them to being with me." Feelings of helplessness were mingled with long-dammed-up rage against the mother who had not been available to him when he needed her the most. As a result of becoming aware of these feelings, Peter could rid himself of a symptom that had tormented him for a long time; its point was now easy to understand. His relationships to women changed as his compulsion first to conquer and then to desert them disappeared.

Peter experienced his early feelings of helplessness, of anger, and of being at the mercy of his mostly absent mother in a manner that he could not previously have remembered. One can only remember what has been consciously experienced. But the emotional world of a tormented child is itself the result of a selective process that has eliminated the most important elements. These early feelings, joined with the pain of being unable to understand what is going on—which is part of the earliest period of childhood—are consciously experienced for the first time during therapy.

It is like a miracle each time to see how much authenticity and integrity have survived behind dissimulation, denial, and self-alienation, and how they can reappear as soon as the patient finds access to the feelings. Nevertheless, it would be wrong to imply that there is a fully developed, true self consciously hidden behind the false self. The important point is that the child does not know what he is hiding. Karl, age forty-two, expressed this in the following way:

> I lived in a glass house into which my mother could look at any time. In a glass house, however, you cannot conceal anything without giving yourself away, except by hiding it under the ground. And then you cannot see it yourself, either.

An adult can be fully aware of his feelings only if he had caring parents or caregivers. People who were abused and neglected in childhood are missing this capacity and are therefore never overtaken by unexpected emotions. They will admit only those feelings that are accepted and approved by their inner censor, who is their parents' heir. Depression and a sense of inner emptiness are the price they must pay for this control. The true self cannot communicate because it has remained unconscious, and therefore undeveloped, in its inner prison. The company of prison warders does not encourage lively development. It is only after it is liberated that the self begins to be articulate, to grow, and to develop its creativity. Where there had been only fearful emptiness or equally frightening grandiose fantasies, an unexpected wealth of vitality is now discovered. This is not a homecoming, since this home has never before existed. It is the creation of home.

## THE THERAPIST'S HISTORY

It is often said that psychotherapists suffer from an emotional disturbance. My purpose so far has been to clarify the extent to which this assertion can be shown to have a basis in experience. The therapist's sensibility, empathy, responsiveness, and powerful "antennae" indicate that as a child he probably used to fulfill other people's needs and to repress his own.

Of course, there is the theoretical possibility that a sensitive child could have had parents who did not need to misuse him—parents who saw him as he really was, understood him, and tolerated and respected his feelings. Although such a child would develop a healthy sense of security, one could hardly expect that he would later take up the profession of psychotherapy; that he would cultivate and develop his sensitivity to others to the same extent as those whose parents used them to gratify their own needs; and that he would ever be able to understand sufficiently—without the basis of experience—what it means to "have killed" one's self.

I think that our childhood fate can indeed enable us to practice psychotherapy, but only if we have been given the chance, through our own therapy, to live with the reality of our past and to give up the most flagrant of our illusions. This means tolerating the knowledge that, to avoid losing the "love" of our parents, we were compelled to gratify their unconscious needs at the cost of our own emotional development. It also means being able to experience the resentment and mourning aroused by our parents' failure to fulfill our primary needs. If we have never consciously lived through this despair and the resulting rage, and have therefore never been able to work through it, we will be in danger of transferring this situation, which then would remain unconscious, onto our patients. It would not be surprising if our unconscious need should find no better way than to make use of a weaker person. Most readily available for exploitation are one's own children or one's patients, who at times are as obedient and as dependent on their therapists as children are on their parents.

A patient with "antennae" for his therapist's unconscious will react promptly. If he senses that it is important to his therapist to have patients who soon become autonomous and behave with self-confidence, he will quickly feel himself autonomous and react accordingly. He can do that; he can do anything that is expected of him. But because this autonomy is not genuine, it soon ends in depression. True autonomy is preceded by the experience of being dependent. True liberation can be found only beyond the deep ambivalence of infantile dependence.

When he presents material that fits the therapist's knowledge, concepts, and skills—and therefore also his expectations—the patient satisfies his therapist's wish for approval, echo, understanding, and for being taken seriously. In this way the therapist exercises the same sort of unconscious manipulation as that to which he was exposed as a child. A child can never see through *unconscious manipulation*. It is like the air he breathes; he knows no other, and it appears to him to be the only breathable air.

What happens if we don't recognize the harmful quality of this air, even in adulthood? We will pass this harm on to others, while pretending that we are acting only for their own good. The extent of the damage we will do depends on our options. If we became novelists, for instance, we might vaguely sense the abyss of childhood suffering and might describe with some accuracy the parents' hypocrisy and their manipulation of the helpless being who is so dependent on them. If we were unaware of the full impact of such manipulation on ourselves and were perhaps even in denial of precisely what we were describing, then while we would not help our readers understand their past, we would at least not harm them, either.

Having decided to become therapists, however, we must not dispense with facing our own truth. If we do not recognize the harm of the manipulation to which we were subjected as children, we cannot avoid passing it on to our patients. A thorough awareness of our own past and a full understanding of its impact seem to me fundamental prerequisites to being able to help others effectively with their therapy.

Unfortunately, we are very far from this standard, as can clearly be seen in the numerous fashionable, extremely manipulative "therapy" concepts appearing almost daily in our time. The German magazine *Der Spiegel* (November 22, 1993) reported that there are currently more than five hundred therapies in Germany promising to make a person happy and free of symptoms—with the help of blatantly manipulative tricks and medications. Psychologists, psychiatrists, therapists, and counselors are apparently fascinated with methods that range from simple behavioral conditioning to neurolinguistic "miracles." How is this possible? Why do they use these manipulative techniques so eagerly, when they must suspect that their effectiveness is at best short-term? Don't they know that any effectiveness is tied to suggestion? That the strong transference the once-fooled child automatically makes onto the "healer" has nothing to do with real healing? Or do they just not know that healing—*real* healing—is indeed possible?

The parents of these professionals did not waste time with reflection, either. They followed the well-worn path taken by their own parents: They didn't want their child to be a person with his or her own needs; they simply wanted a good boy or a nice girl—and they managed to get what they wanted. But if these good boys and nice girls later become therapists or counselors, it is essential that they not go on unconsciously doing to others what their parents did to them, while pretending to be making them happy. They must realize the price they had to pay for their "happiness"—namely, the denial of their own needs, their own true personality, and their unique history. If they can discover that they were once fooled (consciously or unconsciously, the effect was the same) and exactly how this was done, they will no longer want to make others "happy" by tricking them.

The more insight I gain into the unconscious manipulation of children by their parents, and of patients by their therapists, the more urgent it seems to me that we resolve our repression. Not only as parents but also as therapists, we must be willing to face our history. We must be able to feel and clarify our feelings, to understand their old and recent causes in order to integrate our past experiences. We will then no longer have any need to manipulate our patients but can allow them to become what they really are. Only after painfully experiencing and accepting our own truth can we be free from the hope that we might still find an understanding, empathic "parent"—perhaps in a patient—who will be at our disposal.

This temptation to seek a parent among our patients should not be underestimated; our own parents seldom or never listened to us with such rapt attention as our patients usually do, and they never revealed their inner world to us as clearly and honestly as do our patients at times. Only the never-ending work of mourning can help us from lapsing into the illusion that we have found the parent we once urgently needed—empathic and open, understanding and understandable, honest and available, helpful and loving, feeling, transparent, clear, without unintelligible contradictions. Such a parent was never ours, for a mother can react empathically only to the extent that she has become free of her own childhood; when she denies the vicissitudes of her early life, she wears invisible chains.

Children who are intelligent, alert, attentive, sensitive, and completely attuned to the mother's well-being are entirely at her disposal. Transparent, clear, and reliable, they are easy to manipulate as long as their true self (their emotional world) remains in the cellar of the glass house in which they have to live—sometimes until puberty or until they come to therapy, and very often until they have become parents themselves.

Robert, now thirty-one, could never be sad or cry as a child, without being aware that he was making his beloved mother unhappy and very unsure of herself. The extremely sensitive child felt himself warded off by his mother, who had been in a concentration camp as a child but had never spoken about it. Not until her son was grown up and could ask her questions did she tell him that she had been one of eighty children who had had to watch their parents going into the gas chambers and that not one child had cried. Because "cheerfulness" was the trait that had saved her life in childhood, her own children's tears threatened her equilibrium. Throughout his childhood this son had tried to be cheerful. He could express glimpses of his true self and his feelings only in obsessive perversions, which seemed alien, shameful, and incomprehensible to him until he began to grasp their real meaning.

One is totally defenseless against this sort of manipulation in childhood. The tragedy is that the parents too have no defense against it, as long as they refuse to face their own history. If the repression stays unresolved, the parents' childhood tragedy is unconsciously continued on in their children.

Another example may illustrate this more clearly. A father who as a child had often been frightened by the anxiety attacks of his periodically schizophrenic mother and was never given an explanation enjoyed telling his beloved small daughter gruesome stories. He always laughed at her fears and afterward comforted her with the words: "But it is only a made-up story. You don't need to be scared, you are here with me." In this way he could manipulate his child's fear and have the feeling of being strong. His conscious wish was to give the child something valuable of which he himself had been deprived, namely protection, comfort, and explanations. But what he unconsciously handed on was his own childhood fear, the expectation of disaster, and the unanswered question (also from his childhood): Why does this person I love frighten me so much?

Probably everybody has a more or less concealed inner chamber that she hides even from herself and in which the props of her childhood drama are to be found. Those who will be most affected by the contents of this hidden chamber are her children. When the mother was a child she hardly had a chance to understand what happened; she could only develop symptoms. As an adult in therapy, however, she can resolve these symptoms if she allows herself to feel what they were able to disguise: feelings of horror, indignation, despair, and helpless rage.

Can it be an accident that Heinrich Pestalozzi—who was fatherless from his sixth year onward and emotionally neglected despite the presence of his mother and of a nurse— neglected his only son, although he was capable, on the other hand, of giving orphan children genuine warmth and fatherliness? This son was finally considered to be mentally defective, although he had been an intelligent child.[*] He died at the age of thirty. Both his life and his death caused Pestalozzi much

---

[*]In H. Ganz (1966) we can read: "On the occasion of his father's nameday, the five-year-old Jakobli, who could not write, . . . gaily dictated to his mother: 'I wish my dear Papa . . . that you should see a lot more and I thank you a hundred thousand times for your goodness . . . that you have brought me up so joyfully and lovingly. Now I shall speak from my heart. . . . It makes me terribly happy, if you can say: I have brought my son up to happiness. . . . I am his joy and his happiness. Then shall I first give thanks for what you have done in my life. . . .'" (p. 53)

pain and guilt (Ganz, 1966, Lavater-Sloman, 1977). It was also Pestalozzi who is reputed to have said: "You can drive the devil out of your garden but you will find him again in the garden of your son."

## THE GOLDEN BRAIN

Alphonse Daudet's *Lettres de mon Moulin* includes a story that may sound rather bizarre but nevertheless has much in common with what I have presented here. I shall summarize the story briefly:

> Once upon a time there was a child who had a golden brain. His parents only discovered this by chance when he injured his head and gold instead of blood flowed out. They then began to look after him carefully and would not let him play with other children for fear of being robbed. When the boy was grown up and wanted to go out into the world, his mother said: "We have done so much for you, we ought to be able to share your wealth." Then her son took a large piece of gold out of his brain and gave it to his mother. He lived in great style with a friend who, however, robbed him one night and ran away. After that the man resolved to guard his secret and to go out to work, because his reserves were visibly dwindling. One day he fell in love with a beautiful girl who loved him too, but no more than the beautiful clothes he gave her so lavishly. He married her and was very happy, but after two years she died and he spent the rest of his wealth on her funeral, which had to be splendid. Once, as he was creeping through the streets, weak, poor, and unhappy, he saw a beautiful little pair of boots that would have been perfect for his wife. He forgot that she was dead—perhaps because his emptied brain no longer worked—and entered the shop to buy the boots. But in that very moment he fell, and the shopkeeper saw a dead man lying on the ground.

Daudet, who was to die from an illness of the spinal cord, wrote following this story:

> This story sounds as though it were invented, but it is true from beginning to end. There are people who have to pay for the smallest things in life with their very substance and their spinal cord. That is a constantly recurring pain, and then when they are tired of suffering. . . .

Does not mother love belong to the "smallest," but also indispensable, things in life, for which many people paradoxically have to pay by giving up their living selves?

# 2

# Depression and Grandiosity: Two Related Forms of Denial

## THE VICISSITUDES OF THE CHILD'S NEEDS

Every child has a legitimate need to be noticed, understood, taken seriously, and respected by his mother. In the first weeks and months of life he needs to have the mother at his disposal, must be able to avail himself of her and be mirrored by her. This is beautifully illustrated in one of Donald Winnicott's images: the mother gazes at the baby in her arms, and the baby gazes at his mother's face and finds himself therein . . . provided that the mother is really looking at the unique, small, helpless being and not projecting her own expectations, fears, and plans for the child. In that case, the child would find not himself in his mother's face, but rather the mother's own projections. This child would remain without a mirror, and for the rest of his life would be seeking this mirror in vain.

## Healthy Development

If a child is lucky enough to grow up with a mirroring, available mother who is at the child's disposal—that is, a mother who allows herself to be made use of as a function of the child's development—then a healthy self-feeling can gradually develop in the growing child. Ideally, this mother should also provide the necessary emotional climate and understanding for the child's needs. But even a mother who is not especially warmhearted can make this development possible, if only she refrains from preventing it and allows the child to acquire from other people what she herself lacks. Various studies have shown the incredible ability a child displays in making use of the smallest affective "nourishment" (stimulation) to be found in his surroundings.

I understand a healthy self-feeling to mean the unquestioned certainty that the feelings and needs one experiences are a part of one's self. This certainty is not something one can gain upon reflection; it is there like one's own pulse, which one does not notice as long as it functions normally.

The automatic, natural contact with his own emotions and needs gives an individual strength and *self-esteem.* He may experience his feelings—sadness, despair, or the need for help—without fear of making the mother insecure. He can allow himself to be afraid when he is threatened, angry when his wishes are not fulfilled. He knows not only what he does not want but also what he wants and is able to express his wants, irrespective of whether he will be loved or hated for it.

If a woman is to give her child what he will need throughout his life, it is absolutely fundamental that she not be separated from her newborn, for the hormones that foster and nourish her motherly instinct are released immediately after birth and continue in the following days and weeks as she grows more familiar with her baby. When a newborn is separated from his mother—which was the rule not so long ago in maternity hospitals and still occurs in the majority of cases, out of ignorance and for the sake of convenience—then a great opportunity is missed for both mother and child.

The bonding (through skin and eye contact) between mother and baby after birth stimulates in both of them the feeling that they belong together, a feeling of oneness that ideally has been growing from the time of conception. The infant is given the sense of safety he needs to trust his mother, and the mother receives the instinctive reassurance that will help her understand and answer her child's messages. This initial mutual intimacy can never again be created, and its absence can be a serious obstacle right from the start.

The crucial significance of bonding has only recently been proved scientifically. One hopes that it will soon be taken into account in practice, not only in a few select maternity hospitals but in larger hospitals as well, so that everyone will benefit from it. A woman who has experienced bonding with her child will be in less danger of mistreating him and will be in a better position to protect him from mistreatment by the father and other caregivers such as teachers and babysitters.

Even a woman whose own repressed history has been responsible for a lack of bonding with her child can later help him overcome this deficit, if she comes to understand its significance and resolves her repression through therapy. She will also be able to compensate for the consequences of a difficult birth if she does not minimize their importance and knows that a child who was heavily traumatized at the beginning of his life will be in particular need of care and attention in order to overcome the fears arising out of more recent experiences.

## The Disturbance

What happens if a mother not only is unable to recognize and fulfill her child's needs, but is herself in need of assurance? Quite unconsciously, the mother then tries to assuage her own needs through her child. This does not rule out strong affection; the mother often loves her child passionately, but not in the way he needs to be loved. The reliability, continuity, and constancy that are so important for the child are therefore missing from this exploitative relationship. What is missing above all is the framework within which the child could experience his feelings and emotions. Instead, he develops something the mother needs, and although this certainly saves his life (by securing the mother's or the father's "love") at the time, it may nevertheless prevent him, throughout his life, from being himself.

In such cases the natural needs appropriate to the child's age cannot be integrated, so they are repressed or split off. This person will later live in the past without realizing it and will continue to react to past dangers as if they were present.

People who have asked for my assistance because of their depression have usually had to deal with a mother who was extremely insecure and who often suffered from depression herself. The child, most often an only child or the first-born, was seen as the mother's possession. What the mother had once failed to find in her own mother she was able to find in her child: someone at her disposal who could be used as an echo and could be controlled, who was completely centered on her, would never desert her, and offered her full attention and admiration. If the child's demands became too great (as those of her own mother once did), she was no longer so defenseless: she could refuse to allow herself to be tyrannized; she could bring the child up in such a way that he neither cried nor disturbed

her. At last she could make sure that she received considera-
tion, care, and respect.

Barbara, a mother of four children, at thirty-five had only
scanty memories of her childhood relationship with her
mother. At the beginning of treatment, she described her as an
affectionate, warmhearted woman who spoke to her "openly
about her own troubles" at an early age, who was very concerned for her children, and who sacrificed herself for her family. She was often asked for advice by others within the sect to
which the family belonged. Barbara reported that her mother
had always been especially proud of her. The mother was now
old and an invalid, and the patient was very concerned about
her health. She often dreamed that something had happened to
her mother and woke up with great anxiety.

As a consequence of the emotions that arose in Barbara
through therapy, this picture of her mother changed. Above all,
when memories of toilet-training entered her consciousness,
she experienced her mother as domineering, demanding, controlling, manipulative, cold, stupid, petty, obsessive, touchy,
easily offended, overwrought, false, and hard to please. Many
subsequent childhood memories of her mother confirmed these
characteristics. Barbara was then able to connect with the real
reasons for her long-suppressed anger and to discover what her
mother was really like. She realized that when her mother had
felt insecure in relation to her, she had in fact often been cold
and had treated her badly. The mother's anxious concern for the
child had served to ward off her aggression and envy. Since the
mother had often been humiliated as a child, she needed to be
valued by her daughter.

Barbara experienced in therapy for the first time the agonizing fear and rage she had had to repress when she was ten years
old and came home from school on her mother's birthday to
find her lying on the floor with closed eyes. The child cried

out, thinking her mother was dead. The mother then opened her eyes and said, delighted, "You gave me the most precious birthday gift. Now I know that you love me, that somebody loves me." For decades pity and compassion hindered Barbara from realizing the cruelty with which she had been treated. Triggered by a later event, this memory could finally emerge, accompanied by feelings of rage and indignation.

Gradually, the different pictures of the mother were united into that of a single human being whose weakness, insecurity, and oversensitivity made her do everything she could to keep her child at her disposal. The mother, who apparently functioned well with others, was herself basically still a child in her relationship to her own child. The daughter, on the other hand, took over the understanding and caring role until she discovered, with her own children, her previously ignored needs. Before she recognized the story of her past, she had been compelled to press her children into her service, as her mother had done.

## THE ILLUSION OF LOVE

Over the years, my work has included many initial consultations with people whom I saw for one or two sessions before referring them to a colleague. In these short encounters, the tragedy of an individual history can often be seen with moving clarity. In what is described as depression and experienced as emptiness, futility, fear of impoverishment, and loneliness can usually be recognized the tragic loss of the self in childhood, manifested as the total alienation from the self in the adult.

I have witnessed various mixtures and nuances of so-called narcissistic disturbances. For the sake of clarity, I shall describe two extreme forms, of which I consider one to be the reverse of the other—grandiosity and depression. Behind manifest grandiosity there constantly lurks depression, and behind a depressive mood there often hides an unconscious (or conscious but split off) sense of a tragic history. In fact, grandiosity is the defense against depression, and depression is the defense against the deep pain over the loss of the self that results from denial.

## Grandiosity

The person who is "grandiose" is admired everywhere and needs this admiration; indeed, he cannot live without it. He must excel brilliantly in everything he undertakes, which he is surely capable of doing (otherwise he just does not attempt it). He, too, admires himself, for his qualities—his beauty, cleverness, talents—and for his success and achievements. Beware if one of these fails him, for then the catastrophe of a severe depression is imminent.

It is usually considered normal when sick or aged people who have suffered the loss of much of their health and vitality or women who are experiencing menopause become depressive. There are, however, many people who can tolerate the loss of beauty, health, youth, or loved ones and, although they grieve, do so without depression. In contrast, there are those with great gifts, often precisely the most gifted, who do suffer from severe depression. For one is free from it only when self-esteem is based on the authenticity of one's own feelings and not on the possession of certain qualities.

The collapse of self-esteem in a "grandiose" person will show clearly how precariously that self-esteem has been hanging in the air—"hanging from a balloon," as a patient once dreamed. That balloon flew up very high in a good wind but was suddenly punctured and soon lay like a little rag on the ground, for nothing genuine that could have given inner strength and support had ever been developed.

In a field study conducted at Chestnut Lodge, Maryland, in 1954, the family backgrounds of twelve patients suffering from manic-depressive psychoses were examined. The results strongly confirm the conclusions I have reached, by other means, about the etiology of depression:

> All the patients came from families who were socially isolated and felt themselves to be too little respected in their neighborhood. They therefore made special efforts to increase their prestige with their neighbors through conformity and outstanding achievements. The child who later became ill had been assigned a special role in this effort. He was supposed to guarantee the family honor, and was loved only in proportion to the degree to which he was able to fulfill the demands of this family ideal by *means of his special abilities, talents, his beauty, etc.*[*] If he failed, he was punished by being cold-shouldered or thrown out of the family group, and by the knowledge that he had brought great shame on his people. (Eicke-Spengler 1977, p. 1104.)

With today's mobility of families and family members, adapting to a different ethnic culture is essential to survival, but it is threatening to the child's autonomy. Unfortunately, the only "alternative" seems to be a clinging to, or return to, fundamentalism.

Without therapy, it is impossible for the grandiose person to cut the tragic link between admiration and love. He seeks insatiably for admiration, of which he never gets enough because admiration is not the same thing as love. It is only a substitute gratification of the primary needs for respect, understanding,

---

[*]Italics added.

and being taken seriously—needs that have remained unconscious since early childhood. Often a whole life is devoted to this substitute. As long as the true need is not felt and understood, the struggle for the symbol of love will continue. It is for this very reason that an aging, world-famous photographer who had received many international awards could say to an interviewer, "I've never felt what I have done was good enough." And he does not question why he has felt this way. Apparently, it has never occurred to him that the depression he reports could be related to his fusion with the demands of his parents.

A patient once spoke of the feeling of always having to walk on stilts. Is somebody who always has to walk on stilts not bound to be constantly envious of those who can walk on their own legs, even if they seem to him to be smaller and more "ordinary" than he is himself? And is he not bound to carry pent-up rage within himself, against those who have made him afraid to walk without stilts? He could also be envious of healthy people because they do not have to make a constant effort to earn admiration, and because they do not have to do something in order to impress, one way or the other, but are free to be "average."

The grandiose person is never really free; first, because he is excessively dependent on admiration from others, and second, because his self-respect is dependent on qualities, functions, and achievements that can suddenly fail.

## Depression as the Reverse of Grandiosity

In many of the patients I have known, depression was coupled with grandiosity in many ways.

1. Depression sometimes appeared when grandiosity *broke down* as a result of sickness, disablement, or aging. In the case

of an unmarried woman, external sources of approval gradually dried up as she grew older. She no longer received constant confirmation of her attractiveness, which earlier had served a directly supportive function as a substitute for the missing mirroring by her mother. Superficially, her despair about getting old seemed to be due to the absence of sexual contacts but, at a deeper level, early fears of being abandoned were now aroused, and this woman had no new conquests with which to counteract them. All her substitute mirrors were broken. She again stood helpless and confused, as the small girl once did before her mother's face, in which she found not herself but only her mother's confusion.

Men often experience becoming older in a similar way, even if a new love affair may seem to create the illusion of their youth for a time and may in this way introduce brief manic phases into the early stages of the depression brought to the surface by their aging.

2. In the combination of *alternating phases* of grandiosity and depression, their common ground can be recognized. They are the two sides of a medal that can be described as the "false self," a medal that was once actually won for achievement.

For example, at the height of his success an actor can play before an enthusiastic audience and experience feelings of heavenly greatness and almightiness. Nevertheless, his sense of emptiness and futility, even of shame and anger, can return the next morning if his happiness the previous night was not only due to his creative activity in playing and expressing the part but was also, and above all, rooted in the substitute satisfaction of old needs for echoing, mirroring, and being seen and understood. If his success the previous night serves only to deny childhood frustrations, then, like every substitute, it can bring only momentary satisfaction. In fact, true satisfaction is no longer possible, since the right time for that now lies irrevocably in the past. The former child no longer exists, nor do the former parents. The present parents—if they are still alive—are now old and dependent; they no longer have any power over their son and are perhaps delighted with his success and with his infrequent visits. In the present, the son enjoys success and recognition, but these things cannot offer him more than their present value; they cannot fill the old gap. Again, as long as he is able to deny this need with the help of illusion—that is, with the intoxication of success—the old wound cannot heal. Depression leads him close to his wounds, but only mourning for what he has missed, *missed at the crucial time,* can lead to real healing.[*]

3. Continuous performance of outstanding achievements may sometimes enable a person to maintain the illusion of the constant attention and availability of his parents (whose absence from his early childhood he now denies just as thoroughly as his own emotional reactions). Such a person is usually able to ward off threatening depression with *increased displays of brilliance,* thereby deceiving both himself and those around him. However, he quite often chooses a marriage partner who either already has strong depressive traits or, at least within their marriage, unconsciously takes over and enacts the

---

[*]Let me cite a remark by Igor Stravinsky as an example of successful mourning: "I am convinced that it was my misfortune that my father was spiritually very distant from me and that even my mother had no love for me. When my oldest brother died unexpectedly (without my mother transferring her feelings from him onto me, and my father, also, remaining as reserved as ever), I resolved that one day I would show them. Now this day has come and gone. No one remembers this day but me, who am its only remaining witness." This is in marked contrast to a statement by Samuel Beckett: "One could say that I had a happy childhood, although I showed little talent for being happy. My parents did all that can be done to make a child happy, but I often felt very lonely." Beckett's childhood drama had been fully repressed, and idealization of the parents had been maintained with the help of denial, yet the boundless isolation of his childhood found expression in his plays. (For both quotations see Mueller-Braunschweig, 1974.)

depressive components of the grandiose partner. The depression is thus kept outside, and the grandiose one can look after his "poor" partner, protect her like a child, feel strong and indispensable, and thus gain another supporting pillar for the building of his own personality. Actually, however, that personality has no secure foundation and is dependent on the supporting pillars of success, achievement, "strength," and, above all, the denial of the emotional world of his childhood.

Although the outward picture of depression is quite the opposite of that of grandiosity and has a quality that expresses the tragedy of the loss of self in a more obvious way, they have many points in common:

- A false self that has led to the loss of the potential true self
- A fragility of self-esteem because of a lack of confidence in one's own feelings and wishes
- Perfectionism
- Denial of rejected feelings
- A preponderance of exploitative relationships
- An enormous fear of loss of love and therefore a great readiness to conform
- Split-off aggression
- Oversensitivity
- A readiness to feel shame and guilt
- Restlessness.

## Depression as Denial of the Self

Depression consists of a denial of one's own emotional reactions. This denial begins in the service of an absolutely essential adaptation during childhood and indicates a very early injury. There are many children who have not been free, right from the beginning, to experience the very simplest of feelings, such as discontent, anger, rage, pain, even hunger—and, of course, enjoyment of their own bodies.

Beatrice, fifty-eight, the daughter of missionary parents and a sufferer of deep depression, never knew whether she was hungry or not. Her mother had written proudly in her diary that at the age of three months Beatrice had already learned to *wait* to be fed and to suppress her hunger, without crying. Discontent and anger aroused uncertainty in her mother, and her children's pain made her anxious. Her children's enjoyment of their bodies aroused both her envy and her shame about "what other people would think." Under such circumstances, a child may learn very early in life what she is not supposed to feel.

If we have thrown away the keys to understanding our lives, the causes of depression—as well as those of all suffering, illness, and healing—must remain a mystery to us, regardless of whether we call ourselves psychiatrists or authorities in the sciences or both. When psychiatrists with decades of experience have never dared to face their own reality and have instead spent their time (and their patients' time) talking about "dysfunctional families," they will need a concept like a "Higher Power" or God to explain to themselves the "miracle" of healing. They will then behave like people who are faithfully trying to follow a map, without realizing that the first step they took was in the wrong direction. Because they have lost the way from the very start, their "scientific" fidelity to the map doesn't give them the expected results and doesn't take them where they want to go. I would like to illustrate this with an example.

A psychiatrist whose book was sent to me by a reader argues that mistreatment, neglect, and exploitation in childhood cannot be the only causes of psychic illnesses. There must, he feels, be other, irrational reasons that can explain why one person apparently escapes the catastrophic effects of abuse—or at least is able to heal more quickly—while another seems to suffer more intensely or for a longer time. It must, he suspects, be "grace."

He reports the story of a patient who lived with his single mother in extreme poverty for the first year of his life and who was then taken away from her by the authorities. He was placed in one foster home after another, and in all of them the child was severely mistreated. But when he became a psychiatric patient, he healed faster than many others with less obvious stories of abuse. How could this man, who had endured unspeakable cruelty in his childhood and youth, liberate himself so readily from his symptoms? Was it with God's help?

Many people love this type of explanation, without raising a very significant question: Shouldn't we ask why God was willing neither to help other patients of this psychiatrist nor to help this man when he was being beaten mercilessly as a child? Was it really God's grace that helped him as an adult, or is the explanation more prosaic? If this man had a mother who, in spite of her poverty, gave him real love, respect, protection, and security in his first year, he would have had a better start in life and would then have been better able to deal with later abuse than would a patient whose integrity was injured from the first day of her life—as was Beatrice, for instance.

Beatrice was not physically mistreated in her youth. She did, however, have to learn as a small infant how to make her mother happy by not crying, by not being hungry—by not having any needs at all. She suffered first from anorexia and then, throughout her adult life, from severe depression. Psychiatrists are denying this type of damage when they talk about "grace" and other "spiritual" qualities. In order to acknowledge the consequences of such early, hidden trauma, they would first have to do some hard work on themselves. Once they become willing to face the facts—their *own* facts—they will lose interest in teaching others about grace and other "mysteries" in the name of science.

Clinging uncritically to traditional ideas and beliefs often serves to obscure or deny real facts of our life history. Without free access to these facts, the sources of our ability to love remain cut off. No wonder, then, that even well-intended moral appeals—to be loving, caring, generous, and so forth—are fruitless. We cannot really love if we are forbidden to know our truth, the truth about our parents and caregivers as well as about ourselves. We can only try *to behave as if we were loving*. But this hypocritical behavior is the opposite of love. It is confusing and deceptive, and it produces much helpless rage in the deceived person. This rage must be repressed in the presence of the pretended "love," especially if one is dependent, as a child is, on the person who is masquerading in this illusion of love.

We could make great progress in becoming more honest, respectful, and conscious, thus less destructive, if religious leaders could acknowledge and respect these simple psychological laws. Instead of ignoring them, they should open their eyes to the vast damage produced by hypocrisy, in families and in society as a whole. Vera's letter to me, from which she asked me to quote, gives a clear example of this confusion and damage. And Maja's history shows how spontaneous love for a child eventually became possible for her, once the repression of her past had been resolved. Vera, age fifty-two, wrote:

I had been a chronic alcoholic since adolescence, and I finally became sober thanks to Alcoholics Anonymous. I was so grateful for this liberation from my alcohol addiction that I attended every weekly meeting for eleven years. For a long time I managed to ignore and override my own critical thoughts concerning the moral issues represented there. I even succeeded at first in not taking any notice of the serious illness I began to develop (eventually diagnosed as multiple sclerosis) and in making light of the symptoms. It was only when my depressive moods became longer and refused to disappear that I began to face my truth.

From your books I knew about Stettbacher's method, and I had already read his book, but it had not touched me that time at all. Now I started to work systematically with his method. It was very hard at first. When I succeeded in retrieving some repressed memories, they were close to unbearable. I wanted to stop. But my curiosity and my pain were stronger than my fear, and I decided to continue. During the first year of intensive work some of my symptoms disappeared. Now, after three years of work with this method, I understand that these symptoms *had* to develop in order to wake me from my dangerous sleep so that I could finally take seriously my feelings, perceptions, and thoughts.

I knew, for instance, that I had often become angry when "unconditional love" was discussed in the group meetings. I was apparently supposed to perceive and appreciate that all the members were giving me unconditional love. I was supposed to learn to trust them, and I felt guilty if I couldn't. It was explained to me that I could not trust and believe that love existed at all because I hadn't received love in my dysfunctional family of origin. I took these explanations for granted because I was longing so much for love and wanted to believe that I actually was loved. I was unable to question what I was told, because hypocrisy had been the food I was fed daily by my mother—it was so familiar to me, though never questionable. But today I do question things that do not make sense to me.

Today I would say: Only a child needs (and absolutely needs) unconditional love. We must give it to the children who are entrusted to us. We must be able to love and accept them whatever they do, not only when they smile charmingly but also when they cry and scream. But to pretend to love an adult unconditionally—that is, independently of his or her deeds—would mean that we should love even a cold serial murderer or a notorious liar if only he joins our group. Can we do that? Should we even try? Why? For whose sake? If we say that we love an adult unconditionally, we only prove our blindness and/or dishonesty. Nothing else.

This is only one of many glimpses through the fog of religious heritage I tolerated in those meetings for much too long. I owe these insights to my lonely work with the Four-Step Method. This ability to reason developed in me as I talked to my parents in my inner dialogue. It never occurred to me to have any conscious doubts when I was sitting in the meetings. I so desperately wanted to be loved—and that meant, of course, to comply, to be obedient. It was actually a very, very *conditional* "love" that was being offered there.

Vera is right. As adults we don't need unconditional love, not even from our therapists. This is a childhood need, one that can never be fulfilled later in life, and we are playing with illusions if we have never mourned this lost opportunity. But there are other things we can get from good therapists: reliability, honesty, respect, trust, empathy, understanding, and an ability to clarify their emotions so that they need not bother us with them. If a therapist promises unconditional love, we must protect ourselves from him, from his hypocrisy and lack of awareness.

Vera was able to make an important discovery during her lonely work, thanks not only to the method she used but also to her determination to find the truth and not allow herself to be deceived again. The changes in her body, once she paid attention to it, supported her on her path.

Maja, thirty-eight, came to me several weeks after the birth of her third child and told me how free and alive she felt with this baby, quite in contrast to the way she had felt with her two previous children. With them she had constantly felt that excessive demands were being made upon her, that she was a prisoner, and that the babies were taking advantage of her and exploiting her. Thus she rebelled against their justified demands and, at the same time, felt that this was very bad of her: as in depression, she was separated from her true self. She thought these earlier reactions might actually have been rebellion against her mother's demands, for this time she was experiencing nothing of the sort. The love she had then struggled to feel now came of its own accord. She could enjoy her unity with this child and with herself. Then she spoke of her mother in the following words:

I was the jewel in my mother's crown. She often said: "Maja can be relied upon, she will cope." And I did cope. I brought up the smaller children for her so that she could get on with her professional career. She became more and more famous, but I never saw her happy. How often I longed for her in the evenings. The little ones cried and I comforted them but I myself never cried. Who would have wanted a crying child? I could only win my mother's love if I was competent, understanding, and controlled, if I never questioned her actions or showed her how much I missed her; that would have limited her freedom, which she needed so much. It would have turned her against me. At that time, nobody ever would have thought that this quiet, competent, useful Maja could be so lonely and have suffered so much. What could I do but be proud of my mother and help her? The deeper the hole in my mother's heart, the bigger the jewels in her crown needed to be. My poor mother needed these jewels because, at bottom, all her activity served only to suppress something in herself, perhaps a longing, I don't know. . . . Perhaps *she* would have discovered it if she had been fortunate enough to be a mother in more than a biological sense.

And how all of this repeated itself with Peter! How many empty hours my child had to spend with mother substitutes so that I could get my "freedom," which only took me further away from him and from myself. Now I know that I was looking for a way to avoid my feelings when I deserted him— without seeing what I was doing to him, because I had never been able to experience my own sense of being deserted. Only now do I begin to realize what motherhood without crown or jewels or a halo can be like.

A German women's magazine (which tries to speak openly of truths that have been taboo) published a reader's letter in which the tragic story of her experience of motherhood was told without disguise. Her report ends with the following passage:

And then the breast-feeding! The baby was put to the breast all wrong and soon my nipples were all bitten. God, how that hurt. Just two hours and then it was back: another one . . . the same. While it was sucking there, I was crying and swearing above it. It was so terrible that soon I couldn't eat any more and had a temperature of 40 degrees [Celsius]. Then I was allowed to wean and suddenly felt better. It was a long time before I noticed any maternal feelings. I wouldn't have minded if the baby had died. And everybody expected me to be happy. In despair I telephoned a friend who said that I'd get fond of him in time through being busy with him and having him around all the time. But that did not happen either. I only *began to be fond* of him when I could go back to work and only saw him when I came home, as a *distraction and toy,* so to speak. But quite honestly, a little dog would have done just as well. Now that he is gradually getting bigger and I see that *I can train him and that he is devoted to me and trusts me,* I am beginning to develop *tender feelings* for him and am glad that he is there.*

I have written all this because I think it is a good thing that someone should, at last, say that there is no such thing as mother love—not to speak of a maternal instinct. (*Emma,* July 1977)

This woman could not really experience either her own tragedy or that of her child, since her own emotionally inaccessible childhood was the real beginning and the actual key to this story. Her negative statement is thus incorrect. In truth,

*Italics added.

mother love and maternal instinct do exist; we can see them at work when we observe animals that have not been mistreated by human beings. Women, too, are born with instinctual programming to love, support, protect, and nurture their children and to derive pleasure from doing so. But we are robbed of these instinctual abilities if we are exploited in our childhood for the substitute gratification of our parents' needs. Fortunately, however, as Johanna's story shows, we can also restore these abilities as soon as we are determined to face our truth.

Johanna, age twenty-five, began her Four-Step self-therapy just before she became pregnant. She was well prepared for the birth and enjoyed bonding with her healthy newborn. She was happy that her milk was abundant and was anticipating the joys of breast-feeding when suddenly, apparently without reason, her breasts became hard and painful and she developed a high fever. She was distraught when the nurse had to feed the baby with a bottle.

In her nightmares during the fever states, Johanna dreamed repeatedly and with many details of being sexually exploited in infancy by both of her parents and their friend. Thanks to the feelings that had been awakened in her self-therapy, she was able to feel her rage about the rape, the betrayal, and the damage to her instinctual capacity to fulfill her child's needs. This last of her parents' crimes was what made her most furious. She said later: "They robbed me of my motherhood when I was three months old. Because of what happened then, I was unable to breast-feed my child, although I wanted it so desperately." It took a long time for her to confront her parents in an inner dialogue, to express all the feelings of rage and indignation that were stored up in her body, and finally to overcome the effects of these violations.

Even before this complete healing could take place, Johanna's willingness to face the horrible truth brought about a decrease in her temperature and an improvement in the condition of her breasts. She was able to feed her baby, who very quickly learned to dispense with the bottle. This came as a surprise to the nurse, who had been absolutely certain it "would never work."

Johanna was happy with her child. She enjoyed being able to love, to protect, to nurture, to hold her child, and to guess his needs. But this well-being was again and again interrupted by phases of doubt and fear that she would be confronted by catastrophic events if she continued to do what was simply a pleasure for her. As she had studied psychology, she wondered whether she suffered from an obsession and was just compelled to use her son for her own satisfaction, out of pure egoism. This painful self-condemnation was supported by her friends, who warned her about too much "permissiveness" and instructed her that a child needs to learn his limits from the beginning. Otherwise he will become a tyrant. Although Johanna rejected these opinions for a long time, with her own child she was surprisingly sensitive to them and became quickly confused.

The Four-Step Therapy helped her to find orientation, again and again. And she found repeatedly in the fourth step how important it was to her just being able to love, to express her love without being afraid that she could be betrayed, exploited, violated. This love gave her the feeling of being whole, as she had been before her integrity had been injured. In her confrontation with her parents in the third step, she said:

> I love Michael, I want to love him. My soul needs this love like my body needs air. But I am so often in danger of suppressing my need with the help of my whole energy and my intellect. I think that I must "free" myself from this attachment, that it is "wrong." Why? How have you brought me to feel these silly things? Maybe, by teaching me so early that a

child doesn't deserve respect, that he is not a person, that he can be used as a toy to play with, that he can be ignored, mistreated, threatened without any consequences. It is this message, your message, that confuses me still from time to time, that makes me sometimes feel overdemanded and under stress, but I still do not dare to feel my rage toward you and become impatient with Michael. It seems easier to feel that it is Michael who hinders me to be free because he needs so much of my time. But it is not him. I only need to look at his eyes, to see his innocence and his honesty, and I know it: I have used him again as a scapegoat to protect you.

A loved child learns from the beginning what love is. A neglected, exploited, and mistreated child like me can't know it; she never had the chance to learn it. But I do learn it now, from Michael, very slowly, and I know that I will succeed, in spite of your messages. Because now I know how much I need to be able to love and no longer to have doubts about my ability.

I think that Johanna's struggle for her true feelings saved not only her child's future but also her own. Ann's story shows what can happen later to a molested child without this struggle, without therapy. Ann, fifty years old, wrote to me a few days before her death:

I had a visit from my adult children today and realized for the first time in my life that I have been loved by them, the whole time, and I never felt this love until today. I have abandoned them so often with various men and have actually been fleeing constantly from my children and my love for them, from my true feelings, into sexual pleasure with men who caused me so much pain and never gave me what I really needed: love, understanding, acceptance. As an infant I was conditioned by my father to look for pleasure connected with pain and rage and to avoid true love. Was it not a perversion? I was unable to escape it my whole life. And now, I can see it, but it is too late.

It was too late because, although Ann could see and understand what had happened to her, she was able to feel the rage and indignation only toward her partners, not toward her father. As she wrote in her letter, she still "loved" and respected him.

## DEPRESSIVE PHASES DURING THERAPY

A grandiose person will look for a therapist only if depressive episodes come to his aid and force him to do so. As long as the grandiose defense is effective, this form of disturbance exerts no pressure through visible suffering, except when other members of the family (spouse or children) have to seek psychotherapeutic help for depression or psychosomatic disorders. In therapeutic work, we encounter grandiosity only when it is coupled with depression. On the other hand, we see depression in almost all our patients, either in the form of a manifest illness or in distinct phases of depressive moods. These phases can have different functions.

### Signal Function

It happens quite often that a patient arrives complaining of depression and later leaves the consulting room in tears but much relieved and free from depression. Perhaps this patient has been able to experience a long-pent-up rage against her parent or has been able to express her mistrust. Perhaps she has felt for the first time her sadness over the many lost years of her life during which she did not really live or has vented her anger over the impending holidays and separation from her therapist. It is irrelevant which of these feelings are coming to the fore; the important thing is that they can be experienced and that access is thereby allowed to repressed memories. The depression was a signal of both their proximity and their denial. A present event enabled the feelings to break through, and then the depression disappeared. Such a mood can be an indication that parts of the self that had been rejected (feelings, fantasies, wishes, fears) have become stronger, without being discharged in grandiosity.

## Suppression of Essential Needs

Mary, age thirty-nine, would sometimes leave a session feeling content and understood after having come close to the core of her self. But then she would distract herself with a party or something equally unimportant to her at that moment, which would make her feel lonely and inadequate again. After a few days she would complain of self-alienation and emptiness, of once more having lost the way to herself. In this way she was actively, though unconsciously, provoking a situation that could demonstrate what used to happen to her as a child: Whenever she began, through her imaginative play, to have a true sense of herself, her parents would ask her to do something "more sensible"—to achieve something—and her inner world, which was just beginning to unfold, would be closed off to her. She reacted to this interference by withdrawing her feelings and becoming depressed, because she could not take the risk of a normal reaction—rage, perhaps.

If as an adult this person allows herself to face such reminders and work with them in the Four Steps, she will be able to feel the old rage (in Step 2), rebel against the way she was treated (in Step 3), and find the repressed need (in Step 4). The depression will then disappear, because its defensive function is no longer needed. She will no longer have to flee into such activities as parties if she allows herself to know what she really needs at that very moment—possibly to *avoid* distraction and spend some time alone with herself in her plight.

## The Accumulation of Strong, Hidden Feelings

Depressive phases may last several weeks before strong emotions from childhood break through. It is as though the depression has held back the affect. When it can be experienced, insight and associations related to the repressed scenes follow, often accompanied by significant dreams. The patient feels fully alive again until a new depressive phase signals something new. This may be expressed in the following fashion: "I no longer have a feeling of myself. How could it happen that I should lose myself again? I have no connection with what is within me. It is all hopeless . . . it will never be any better. Everything is pointless. I am longing for my former sense of being alive." An emotional outbreak may follow, accompanied by strong, legitimate reproaches, and only after this outbreak will a new link with repressed experience become clear and new vitality be felt. As long as these reproaches are directed toward those who are responsible for harming us, a great relief is the result. If, however, they are unjust, or transferred onto innocent persons, the depression will continue until full clarification becomes possible.

## Confronting the Parents

There will be times of depressive moods even after a person has started to resist the demands of his parents, as many things remain unconscious, repressed. He may, for example, resist their demands for achievement, although he has not yet fully freed himself from them. He will land again in the dead end of making pointlessly excessive demands upon himself and will become aware that he is doing so only when a depressive mood rises. He might, for example, report the following experience:

The day before yesterday I was so happy. My work went easily—I was able to do more work for the exam than I had
planned for the whole week. Then I thought I must take
advantage of this good mood and do another chapter in the
evening. I worked all evening but without any enthusiasm,
and the next day I couldn't do any more. I felt like such an
idiot. Nothing stayed in my head. I didn't want to see anyone,
either; it felt like the depressions I used to have. Then I
"turned the pages back" and found the very moment it had
begun. I had spoiled my pleasure as soon as I made myself do
more and more. But why? Then I remembered how my mother
used to say: "You have done that beautifully, now you could
surely do this, too. . . ." I got very angry and left the books
alone. Then, later, I trusted myself to know when I was ready
to work again. And, of course, I did know. But the depression
went away sooner—at the point when I got angry and realized
how, and why, I had once again exceeded my limits.

## THE INNER PRISON

Everyone probably knows about depressive moods from personal experience since they may be expressed as well as hidden
by psychosomatic suffering. It is easy to notice, if we pay attention, that they hit almost with regularity—whenever we suppress an impulse or an unwanted emotion. Then, suddenly, a
depressive mood will stifle all spontaneity. If an adult, for
example, cannot experience grief when he loses somebody dear
to him but tries to distract himself from his sadness, or if he
suppresses* and hides from himself his indignation over an idealized friend's behavior out of fear of losing his friendship, he
must reckon with the probability of depression (unless his
grandiose defense is constantly at his disposal). When he
begins to pay attention to these connections, he can benefit

---

*Suppression is a *conscious* act, in contrast to repression.

from his depression and use it to learn the truth about himself, guided by the Four-Step Method.

Once we have experienced a few times that the break-through of intense early-childhood feelings (characterized by the specific quality of noncomprehension) can relieve a long period of depression, this experience will bring about a gradual change in our way of approaching "undesired" feelings—painful feelings, above all. We discover that we are no longer compelled to follow the former pattern of disappointment, suppression of pain, and depression, since we now have another possibility of dealing with disappointment: namely, experiencing the pain. In this way we at last gain access to our earlier experiences—to the parts of ourselves and our fate that were previously hidden from us.

A child does not yet have this possibility open to her. She cannot yet see through her mechanism of self-deception, and, on the other hand, she is far more threatened than an adult by the intensity of her feelings if she does not have a supportive, empathic environment. Moreover, she can be in actual external danger. In contrast to the child, the adult is not in danger when she dares to feel, although she may, of course, fear the danger of her former situation (for the first time) as long as the reasons for her fear remain unconscious.

The extreme intensity of childhood feeling is to be found nowhere else, except in puberty. The recollection of the pains of puberty, however—of not being able to understand or to place our own impulses—is usually more accessible than the earliest traumas, which are often hidden behind the picture of an idyllic childhood or even behind an almost complete amnesia. This is perhaps one reason why adults less often look back nostalgically to the time of their puberty than to that of their childhood. The mixture of longing, expectation, and fear of disappointment that for most people accompanies the remembrance of festivities from childhood can perhaps be explained by their search for the intensity of feeling they lost back then.

It is precisely because a child's feelings are so strong that they cannot be repressed without serious consequences. The stronger a prisoner is, the thicker the prison walls have to be, and unfortunately these walls also impede or completely prevent later emotional growth. In the closing phase of his therapy with me, a patient described the new understanding that came with the dismantling of his inner wall:

> It was not the beautiful or pleasant feelings that gave me new insight, but the ones against which I had fought most strongly: feelings that made me experience myself as shabby, petty, mean, helpless, humiliated, demanding, resentful, or confused; and, above all, sad and lonely. It was precisely through these experiences, which I had shunned for so long, that I became certain that I now understand something about my life, stemming from the core of my being, something that I could not have learned from any book!

This patient was describing the process of gaining insight. Interpretations from therapists who ignore their own childhood history can disturb, hamper, and delay this process, or even prevent it or reduce it to mere intellectual insight. A person seeking help is all too ready to give up his own pleasure in discovery and self-expression and accommodate himself to his therapist's concepts, out of fear of losing the latter's affection, understanding, and empathy, for which he has been waiting all his life. Because of his early experiences with his mother, he cannot believe that this need not happen. If he gives way to this fear and adapts himself, the therapy slides over into the realm of the false self, and the true self remains hidden and undeveloped. It is therefore extremely important that the therapist not allow his own needs to impel him to formulate connections that the patient himself is discovering with the help of his own feelings. Otherwise he is in danger of behaving like a friend who brings a good meal to a prisoner in his cell, at the precise moment when that prisoner has the chance to escape— perhaps to spend his first night hungry and without shelter, but in freedom nevertheless. Since this first step into unknown territory would require a great deal of courage, the prisoner may comfort himself with his food and shelter and thus miss his chance and stay in prison.

Recognizing the fragility of the healing process obviously does not mean that the therapist must adopt a mostly silent and hurtful attitude, but merely that he must exercise care in this respect. It will then become possible for old, unremembered situations to be experienced consciously in their full tragedy for the first time and be mourned at last. Apparently, for many people that works more effectively without the help of therapists.

It is part of the dialectic of the grieving process that the experience of pain both encourages and is dependent on self-discovery. If the psychotherapist invites the patient to share in his own "grandeur," or if the patient is enabled to feel powerful as part of a therapeutic group, he will experience relief from his depression for a while, but the disturbance will still exist, appearing in a different guise for a time. Because grandiosity is the counterpart of depression *within* the narcissistic disturbance, the achievement of freedom from *both* forms of disturbance is hardly possible without deeply felt mourning about the situation of the former child. This ability to grieve—that is, to give up the illusion of his "happy" childhood, to feel and recognize the full extent of the hurt he has endured—can restore the depressive's vitality and creativity and free the grandiose person from the exertions of and dependence on his Sisyphean task. If a person is able, during this long process, to experience the reality that he was never loved as a child for what he was but was instead needed and exploited for his achievements, success, and good qualities—and that he sacrificed his childhood for this form of love—he will be very deeply shaken, but one day he will feel the desire to end these efforts. He will discover in himself a need to live according to his true self and no longer be forced to earn "love" that always leaves him empty-handed, since it is given to his false self—something he has begun to identify and relinquish.

The true opposite of depression is neither gaiety nor absence of pain, but vitality—the freedom to experience spontaneous feelings. It is part of the kaleidoscope of life that these feelings are not only happy, beautiful, or good but can reflect the entire range of human experience, including envy, jealousy, rage, disgust, greed, despair, and grief. But this freedom cannot be achieved if its childhood roots are cut off. Our access to the true self is possible only when we no longer have to be afraid of the intense emotional world of early childhood. Once we have experienced and become familiar with this world, it is no longer strange and threatening. We no longer need to keep it hidden behind the prison walls of illusion. We know now who and what caused our pain, and it is exactly this knowledge that gives us freedom at last from the old pain.

A good deal of advice for dealing with depression (for example, turning aggression from the inner to the outer world) has a clearly manipulative character. Some psychiatrists, for instance, suggest that the therapist should demonstrate to the patient that his hopelessness is not rational or make him aware of his oversensitivity. I think that such procedures will not only strengthen the false self and emotional conformity but will reinforce the depression as well. If therapists want to avoid doing so, they must take *all* of the patients' feelings seriously. How often depressive patients are aware that they have reacted oversensitively, and how much they reproach themselves for it. It is precisely their oversensitivity, shame, and self-reproach that form a continuous thread in their lives, unless they learn to understand to what these feelings actually relate. The more unrealistic such feelings are and the less they fit present reality, the more clearly they show that they are concerned with unremembered situations from the past that are still to be discovered. If the feeling that begins to arise is not experienced but reasoned away, the discovery cannot take place, and depression will triumph.

Pia, age forty, after a long depressive phase accompanied by suicidal thoughts, was at last able to experience and justify her long-suppressed rage toward her father, who had severely mistreated her. This experience was followed immediately not by visible relief, but by a period full of grief and tears. At the end of this period she said:

> The world has not changed. There is so much evil and meanness all around me, and I see it even more clearly than before. Nevertheless, for the first time I find life really worth living. Perhaps this is because, for the first time, I have the feeling that I am really living my own life. And that is an exciting adventure. On the other hand, I can understand my suicidal ideas better now, especially those I had in my youth—when it seemed pointless to carry on—because in a way I had always been living a life that wasn't mine, that I didn't want, and that I was ready to throw away.

## A SOCIAL ASPECT OF DEPRESSION

One might ask whether adaptation must necessarily lead to depression. Is it not possible, and do we not sometimes see, that emotionally conforming individuals may live quite happily? There were perhaps many such examples in the past.

Within a culture that was shielded from other value systems, an adapted individual was, of course, not autonomous. He did not have an individual sense of identity (in our sense) that could have given him support, but he felt supported by the group. Today it is hardly possible for any group to remain completely isolated from others with different values. The individual must therefore find his support within himself if he is to avoid becoming the victim of various interests and ideologies.

The so-called therapeutic groups try to but cannot provide or replace this maturational process. Their goal is to "empower" their members by providing them with support and a sense of belonging. Since the suppression of childhood feelings is the rule within these groups, however, the individual's depression cannot be resolved. Moreover, a person can become addicted to the group itself, as the group provides the *illusion* that the unmet needs of the former child can eventually be fulfilled (by the group) in the adult. With such illusions, no one can truly heal. The strength within ourselves—through access to our own real needs and feelings and the possibility of expressing them—is crucially important for us if we want to live without depression and addiction.

Some children have latent powers to resist adaptation and become partially adapted. Older children, particularly as they reach puberty, may attach themselves to new values, which are often opposed to those of the parents. An adolescent may accept and conform to the ideals of a group of youths just as he did to those of his parents when he was younger. But since this attempt is not rooted in an awareness of his own true needs and feelings, he is again giving up and denying his true self in order to be accepted and loved, this time by a peer group. His renewed sacrifice will therefore not relieve his depression. He is not really himself, nor does he know or love himself: Everything he undertakes is done in hope of making somebody love him in the way he once, as a child, so urgently needed to be loved; but what could not be experienced at the appropriate time in the past can never be attained later on.

There are innumerable examples of this dilemma. I will describe two of them:

1. Paula, age twenty-eight, wanted to free herself from her patriarchal family in which the mother was completely subjugated by the father. She married a submissive man and seemed to behave differently from her mother. Her husband allowed her to bring her lovers into the house. She did not permit herself any feelings of jealousy or tenderness and wanted to have relations with a number of men without any emotional ties, so that she could feel as autonomous as a man. Her need to be "progressive" went so far that she allowed her partners to abuse and humiliate her, and she suppressed all her feelings of mortification and anger in the belief that her behavior made her modern and free from prejudice. In this way she unconsciously carried over into these relationships both her childhood obedience and her mother's submissiveness. At times she suffered from severe depression, so she entered therapy, which enabled her to feel how much she suffered because of the passiveness of her mother, who tolerated the abusive father without the slightest opposition. Confronting the pain of not having been protected by her indifferent, defensive mother eventually helped Paula to stop creating her mother's self-destructive attitude in her own relationships with men and to allow herself to love people who deserved her love.

2. Amar, now forty, grew up in an African family, alone with his mother after his father died when he was still a very small boy. His mother insisted on certain conventions and did not allow him to be aware of his needs in any way, let alone express them. On the other hand, she regularly massaged his penis

until puberty, ostensibly on medical advice. As an adult, the son left his mother and her world and married an attractive European with a different background. Due to his repressed history, he chose a woman who not only tormented and humiliated him but also undermined his confidence to an extreme degree, so that he was unable either to stand up to her or to leave her.

This sadomasochistic marriage, like the other example, represents an attempt to break away from the parents' social system with the help of another one. Amar was certainly able to free himself from the mother of his adolescence, but he remained emotionally tied to the mother of his early childhood (and his unconscious memories of her), whose role was taken over by his wife as long as he was not able to experience the feelings from that period. It was terribly painful for him to realize how much he had needed his mother as a child and at the same time had felt abused in his helplessness—how much he had loved her, hated her, and been entirely at her mercy. But as a result of this experience, Amar no longer feared his wife and for the first time dared to see her as she really was.

The child must adapt to ensure the illusion of love, care, and kindness, but the adult does not need this illusion to survive. He can give up his amnesia and then be in a position to determine his actions with open eyes. Only this path will free him from his depression. Both the depressive and the grandiose person *completely deny their childhood reality* by living as though the availability of the parents could still be salvaged: the grandiose person through the illusion of achievement, and the depressive through his constant fear of losing "love." Neither can accept the truth that this loss or absence of love has *already happened* in the past, and that *no effort whatsoever can change this fact.*

## THE LEGEND OF NARCISSUS

The legend of Narcissus actually tells us the tragedy of the loss of the self. Narcissus sees his reflection in the water and falls in love with his own beautiful face, of which his mother was surely proud. The nymph Echo answers the young man's calls because she is in love with his beauty. Echo's answering calls deceive Narcissus. His reflection deceives him as well, since it shows only his perfect, wonderful face and not his inner world, his pain, his history. His back view, for instance, and his shadow remain hidden from him; they do not belong to and are cut off from his beloved reflection.

This stage of rapturous enchantment can be compared to grandiosity, just as the next (the consuming longing for himself) can be likened to depression. Narcissus wanted to be nothing but the beautiful youth; he totally denied his true self. In trying to be at one with the beautiful picture, he gave himself up—to death or, in Ovid's version, to being changed into a flower. This death is the logical consequence of the fixation on the false self. It is not only the "beautiful," "good," and pleasant feelings that make us really alive, deepen our existence, and give us crucial insight, but often precisely the unacceptable and unadapted ones from which we would prefer to escape: helplessness, shame, envy, jealousy, confusion, rage, and grief. These feelings can be experienced in therapy. When they are understood, they open the door to our inner world that is much richer than the "beautiful countenance"!

Narcissus was in love with his idealized picture, but neither the grandiose nor the depressive "Narcissus" can really love himself. His passion for his false self makes impossible not only love for others but also, despite all appearances, love for the one person who is fully entrusted to his care: himself.

# 3

# The Vicious Circle of Contempt

Would not God find a way out, some superior deception
such as the grownups and the powerful always contrived,
producing one more trump card at the last moment, shaming me after all, not taking me seriously, humiliating me
under the damnable mask of kindness?
—HERMANN HESSE, "A CHILD'S HEART"

## HUMILIATION FOR THE CHILD, DISRESPECT FOR THE WEAK, AND WHERE IT GOES FROM THERE

While away on a vacation, I was sorting out my thoughts on the subject of contempt and reading various notes I had made on this theme after individual sessions. Probably sensitized by this preoccupation, I was more than usually affected by an ordinary scene, in no way spectacular or rare. I shall describe it to introduce my observations, for it illustrates, without any danger of indiscretion, some of the insights I have gained in my work.

I was out for a walk and noticed a young couple a few steps ahead, both tall; they had a little boy with them, about two years old, who was running alongside and whining. (We are accustomed to seeing such situations from the adult point of view, but here I want to describe it as experienced by the child.) The two had just bought themselves ice-cream bars on sticks from the kiosk, and were licking them with evident enjoyment. The little boy wanted one, too. His mother said affectionately, "Look, you can have a bite of mine, a whole one is too cold for you." The child did not want just one bite but held out his hand for the whole bar, which his mother took out of his reach again. He cried in despair, and soon exactly the same thing was repeated with his father: "There you are, my pet," said his father affectionately, "you can have a bite of mine." "No, no," cried the child and ran ahead again, trying to distract himself. Soon he came back again and gazed enviously and sadly up at the two grown-ups, who were enjoying their ice cream contentedly. Time and again he held out his little hand for the whole ice-cream bar, but the adult hand with its treasure was withdrawn again.

The more the child cried, the more it amused his parents. It made them laugh, and they hoped to humor him along with their laughter, too: "Look, it isn't so important, what a fuss you are making." Once the child sat down on the ground and began to throw little stones over his shoulder in his mother's direction, but then he suddenly got up again and looked around anxiously, making sure that his parents were still there. When his father had completely finished his ice cream, he gave the stick to the child and walked on. The little boy licked the bit of wood expectantly, looked at it, threw it away, wanted to pick it up again but did not do so, and a deep sob of loneliness and disappointment shook his small body. Then he trotted obediently after his parents.

It seemed clear to me that this little boy was not being frustrated in his "oral wishes," for he was given ample opportunity to take a bite; he was, however, constantly being hurt and frustrated. His wish to hold the ice-cream stick in his hand like the others was not understood. Worse still, it was laughed at; they made fun of his wish. He was faced with two giants who supported each other and who were proud of being consistent while he, quite alone in his distress, could say nothing beyond "no." Nor could he make himself clear to his parents with his gestures (though they were very expressive). He had no advocate. What an unfair situation it is when a child is opposed by two big, strong adults, as by a wall; but we call it "consistency in upbringing" when we refuse to let the child complain about one parent to the other.

Why, indeed, did these parents behave with so little empathy? Why didn't one of them think of eating a little quicker, or even of throwing away half of the ice cream and giving the child the stick with a bit of ice cream left on it? Why did they both stand there laughing, eating so slowly and showing so little concern about the child's obvious distress? They were not unkind or cold parents; the father spoke to his child very tenderly. Nevertheless, at least at this moment, they displayed a lack of empathy.

We can only solve this riddle if we manage to see the parents, too, as insecure children—children who have at last found a weaker creature, in comparison with whom they can now feel very strong. What child has never been laughed at for his fears and been told, "You don't need to be afraid of a thing like that"? What child will then not feel shamed and despised because he could not assess the danger correctly? And will that little person not take the next opportunity to pass these feelings on to a still smaller child? Such experiences come in all shades and varieties. Common to them all is the sense of strength it gives the adult, who cannot control his or her own fears, to face the weak and helpless child's fear and be able to control fear in another person.

No doubt, in twenty years' time—or perhaps earlier if he has younger siblings—our little boy will replay this scene with the ice cream. Now, however, *he* will be in charge, and the other will be the helpless, envious, weak little creature—no longer carried within, but split off and projected outside himself.

Disregard for those who are smaller and weaker is thus the best defense against a breakthrough of one's own feelings of helplessness: it is an expression of this split-off weakness. The strong person who—because he has experienced it—knows that he, too, carries this weakness within himself does not need to demonstrate his strength through contempt.

Many adults first become aware of their feelings of helplessness, jealousy, and loneliness through their own children, since they had no chance to acknowledge and experience these feelings consciously in childhood. I've spoken of the patient Peter who was obsessively forced to make conquests with women, to seduce and then to abandon them, until he was at last able to experience how he himself had repeatedly been abandoned by his mother (pp. 41–43). When he also remembered how he had been laughed at by his parents, he consciously experienced for the first time the feelings of humiliation and mortification that were aroused back then. Until that point, all of these feelings had been completely concealed from his consciousness.

The suffering that was not consciously felt as a child can be avoided by delegating it to one's own children—in much the same way as in the ice cream scene I have just described: "You see, we are big, we may do as we like, but for you it is 'too cold.' You may enjoy yourself as we do only when you get to be big enough." So it is not the frustration of his wish that is humiliating for the child, but the contempt shown for his person. The suffering is accentuated by the parents' demonstrating their "grownupness" to avenge themselves unconsciously on their child for their own earlier humiliation. They encounter their own humiliating past in the child's eyes, and they ward it off with the power they now have. We cannot, simply by an act of will, free ourselves from repeating the patterns of our parents' behavior—which we had to learn very early in life. We become free of them only when we can fully feel and acknowledge the suffering they inflicted on us. We can then become fully aware of these patterns and condemn them unequivocally.

In most societies, little girls suffer additional discrimination because they are girls. Since women, however, usually have control of newborn infants and toddlers, these former little girls can pass on to their children at the most tender age the disrespect from which they once suffered. When that happens, the grown son will idealize his mother, since every human being needs the feeling (and clings to the illusion) that he was really loved; but he will despise other women, upon whom he can take revenge in place of his mother. And the humiliated grown daughter, if she has no other means of ridding herself of her burden, will revenge herself upon her own children. She can do so secretly and without fear of reprisals, for the children have no way of telling anyone, except perhaps later in the form of obsessions or other symptoms, the language of which is sufficiently veiled that the mother is not betrayed.

Disrespect is the weapon of the weak and a defense against one's own despised and unwanted feelings, which could trigger memories of events in one's repressed history. And the fountainhead of all contempt, all discrimination, is the more or less conscious, uncontrolled, and covert exercise of power over the child by the adult. Except in the case of murder or serious bodily harm, this unrestrained use of power is tolerated by society; what adults do to their child's spirit is entirely their own affair, for the child is regarded as the parents' property in the same way as the citizens of a totalitarian state are considered the property of its government. Until we become sensitized to the small child's suffering, this wielding of power by adults will continue to be regarded as a normal aspect of the human condition, for hardly anyone pays attention to it or takes it seriously. Because the victims are "only children," their distress is trivialized. But in twenty years' time these children will be adults who will feel compelled to pay it all back to their own children. They may consciously fight with vigor against cruelty in the world yet carry within themselves an experience of cruelty that they may unconsciously inflict on others. As long as it remains hidden behind their idealized picture of a happy childhood, they will have no awareness of it and will therefore be unable to avoid passing it on.

It is absolutely urgent that people become aware of the degree to which this disrespect of children is persistently transmitted from one generation to the next, perpetuating destructive behavior. Someone who slaps or hits another adult or knowingly insults her is aware of hurting her. Even if he doesn't know why he is doing this, he has some sense of what he is doing. But how often were our parents, and we ourselves toward our own children, unconscious of how painfully, deeply, and abidingly they and we injured a child's tender, budding self?

It is very fortunate when our older children become aware of what we were doing and are able to tell us about it. We are then given the opportunity to recognize our failures and to apologize. Acknowledging what we have done may help them, at last, to throw off the chains of neglect, discrimination, scorn, and misuse of power that have been handed on for generations. When our children can consciously experience their early helplessness and rage, they will no longer need to ward off these feelings, in turn, with the exercise of power over others. In most cases, however, people's childhood suffering remains affectively inaccessible and thus forms the hidden source of new and sometimes very subtle humiliation for the next generation. Various defense mechanisms will help to justify their actions: denial of their own suffering, rationalization (I owe it to my child to bring him up properly), displacement (it is not my father but my son who is hurting me), idealization (my father's beatings were good for me), and more. Above all, there is the mechanism of turning repressed suffering into active behavior. The following examples may illustrate how astonishingly similar the ways are in which people protect themselves against their childhood experiences, despite great differences in personality structure and education.

A thirty-year-old Greek, the son of a peasant and owner of a small restaurant in Western Europe, proudly described how he drinks no alcohol and has his father to thank for this abstinence. Once, at the age of fifteen, he came home drunk and was so severely beaten by his father that he could not move for a week. From that time on he was so averse to alcohol that he could not taste so much as a drop, although his work brought him into constant contact with it. When I heard that he was soon to be married, I asked whether he, too, would beat his children. "Of course," he answered. "Beatings are necessary in bringing up a child properly. They are the best way to make him respect you. I would never smoke in my father's presence, for example—and that is a sign of my respect for him."

This man was neither stupid nor coldhearted, but he had received little schooling. We might therefore nurse the illusion that education could counteract this ongoing process of destroying the spirit. But how does this idea stand up to the next example, which concerns an educated man?

In the seventies, a talented Czech author was reading from his own works in a town in Western Germany. After the reading there followed a discussion with the audience, during which he was asked questions about his life. He answered ingenuously, reporting that despite his former support of the Prague Spring he now had plenty of freedom and could travel frequently in the West. He went on to describe his country's development in recent years. When he was asked about his childhood, his eyes shone with enthusiasm as he talked about his gifted and many-sided father, who encouraged his spiritual development and was a true friend. It was only to his father that he could show his first stories. His father was very proud of him, and even when he beat him as punishment for some misdemeanor reported by the mother, he was proud that his son did not cry. Since tears brought extra blows, the child learned to suppress them and was himself proud that he could make his admired father such a great present with his bravery. This man spoke of these regular beatings as though they were the most normal things in the world (as for him, of course, they were), and then he said: "It did me no harm, it prepared me for life, made me hard, taught me to grit my teeth. And that's why I could get on so well in my profession." And it was also for that reason that he could cooperate so well with the Communist totalitarian regime.

In contrast with this Czech author, the film director Ingmar Bergman spoke on a television program with more understanding and greater—although only intellectual—awareness about the implications of his own childhood, which he described as one long story of humiliation. He related, for example, that if he wet his pants he had to wear a red dress all day so that everybody would know what he had done and he would be ashamed of himself. Bergman, the younger son of a Protestant pastor, described in this television interview a scene that often occurred during his childhood: His older brother has just been beaten by the father. Now their mother is dabbing his brother's bleeding back with cotton, while he himself sits watching. The adult Bergman described this scene without apparent agitation, coldly. One could see him as a child, quietly sitting and watching. He surely did not run away, or close his eyes, or cry. One had the impression that this scene did take place in reality but was at the same time a covering memory for what *he himself* went through. It is unlikely that only his brother was beaten by their father.

Sometimes people are convinced that it was just their siblings who suffered humiliation. Only in therapy can they remember—with feelings of rage and helplessness, of anger and indignation—how humiliated and deserted they felt when they themselves were mercilessly beaten by their beloved father.

Ingmar Bergman, however, had another means, apart from projection and denial, of dealing with his suffering: He could make films and thereby delegate his unfelt feelings to the spectator. We, as the movie audience, are asked to endure those feelings that he, the son of such a father, could not experience overtly but nevertheless carried within himself. We sit before the screen confronted, the way that small boy once was, with all the cruelty "our brother" has to endure, and feel hardly able or willing to take in all this brutality with authentic feelings; we ward them off.

Bergman also spoke regretfully of his failure to see through Nazism before 1945, although as an adolescent he often visited Germany during the Hitler period. I see this blindness as a consequence of his childhood. Cruelty was the familiar air he had breathed from early on, so why should cruelty and disdain for others have caught his attention?

And why have I described three examples of men who were beaten in their childhood? Are these not borderline cases? Do I want to consider only the effects of beatings? By no means. I chose these three cases, although they *may* be crass exceptions, partly because they had not been entrusted to me as secrets but had already been made public; but above all, I meant to show how the impact of even the most severe ill-treatment can remain hidden because of the child's strong tendency to idealization. There is no trial, no advocate, no verdict. Everything remains shrouded in the darkness of the past; and should the facts become known, they appear in the guise of "blessings." If this is so with the most blatant examples of physical mistreatment, then how is emotional torment ever to be exposed, when it is less visible and more easily disputed? Who is likely to take serious notice of subtle discrimination, as in the example of the small boy and the ice cream? But each patient's therapy reveals endless comparable examples.

The parents' exploitation of their child can lead to a long series of sexual and nonsexual abuses, which the child will be able to discover only as an adult in therapy, and often not before he himself is a parent. A father who grew up in a puritanical family may well be inhibited in his sexual relationships in marriage. He may even first dare to look closely at female genitalia, play with them, and feel aroused while he is bathing his small daughter. A mother may perhaps have been shocked as a small girl by the unexpected sight of an erect penis and so developed fear of the male genital, or she may have experienced it as an implement of violence without being able to confide in anyone. Such a mother may now be able to feel she has gained control over her fear in relationship to her tiny son. She may, for example, dry him after his bath in such a manner that he has an erection, which is not dangerous or threatening for her. She may massage her son's penis, right up to puberty, in order "to treat a constriction of his foreskin" without having to be afraid. Protected by the unquestioning love that every child has for his mother, she can carry on with her hesitant sexual exploration, which never had a chance to develop naturally.

What does it mean to the child, however, when her inhibited parents exploit her sexually? Every child seeks loving contact and is happy to get it, but at the same time feels confused, insecure, and afraid when a mixture of feelings is elicited that would not appear spontaneously at this stage in her development. Her fear and confusion are further increased when her own autoerotic activity is punished by the parents' prohibitions or scorn.

There are other ways of exploiting the child apart from the sexual: through brainwashing, for instance, which underlies both the "anti-authoritarian" and the "strict" upbringing. Neither form of rearing takes the child's own needs into account. As soon as he is regarded as a *possession* for which one has a particular *goal,* as soon as one exerts control over him, his natural growth will be violently interrupted.

It is among the commonplaces of education that we often first cut off the living root and then try to replace its natural functions by artificial means. Thus we suppress the child's curiosity, for example (there are questions one should not ask), and then when he lacks a natural interest in learning we offer him special coaching for his scholastic difficulties.

We find a similar example in the behavior of addicts. People who as children successfully repressed their intense feelings often try to regain—at least for a short time—their lost intensity of experience with the help of drugs or alcohol. (See Miller 1983, pp. 107–141).

If we want to avoid unconsciously motivated exploitation and disrespect of the child, we must first gain a conscious awareness of these dangers. Only if we become sensitive to the fine and subtle ways (as well as the more obvious but still denied ways) in which a child may suffer humiliation can we hope to develop the respect for him he will need from the very first day of his life. There are various means of developing this sensitivity. We may, for instance, observe children who are strangers to us and attempt to feel empathy for them in their situation. But we must, above all, come to have empathy for our own fate. Our feelings will always reveal the true story, which no one else knows and which only we can discover.

## WORKING WITH CONTEMPT IN THERAPY

When I worked as a psychoanalyst I was sometimes asked in seminars or supervisors' sessions how one should deal with "undesirable" feelings such as the irritation that patients sometimes arouse in the therapist. A sensitive therapist will of course feel this irritation. Should he suppress it in order to avoid rejecting the patient? But then the patient, too, will sense this suppressed anger, without being able to comprehend it, and will be confused. Should the therapist express it? Doing so may offend the patient and undermine her confidence. The question of how to deal with anger and other unwanted feelings toward the patient no longer needs to be asked if we begin with the assumption that *all* the feelings the patient arouses in her therapist or counselor are part of her unconscious attempt to tell the therapist her story and at the same time to hide it from him. Although the way a patient evokes fear or irritation in the therapist is of course due in part to the patient's history, these feelings can also, in large part, be triggered by the therapist's own past. They should not be warded off, for they always indicate a hidden reality and past knowledge. The therapist must be able to experience them and clear them up. Thanks to the very precise tools contained in the Four Steps, he can find out whether the feelings provoked by the patient are being triggered by his own life history; and if so, he will be able to work on them. The same relates to counselors who work with addicted patients or other victims of sexual or physical childhood mistreatment. Usually, they sense only a trace of their own fear before quickly concealing it with the help of abstract theories, commonplace moral advice, or very often simply authoritarian behavior.

## Damaged Self-Articulation in the Compulsion to Repeat

The newly won capacity to accept her feelings opens the way for the patient's long-repressed needs and wishes to be actualized. Some of these needs cannot be satisfied in reality, since they are related to past situations. The urgent wish for a child, for example, may express among other things the wish to have an available mother. Unfortunately, children are too often wished for only as symbols to meet repressed needs.

All the same, there are needs that can and should be satisfied in the present. Among these is every human being's central need to express herself, to show herself to the world as she really is—in word, in gesture, in behavior, in art—in every genuine expression, beginning with the baby's cry.

For the person who, as a child, had to hide her true feelings from herself and others, this first step into the open produces much anxiety, yet she feels a great need to throw over her former restraints. The first experiences do not always lead to freedom but quite often lead instead to a repetition of the person's childhood situation, in which she will experience feelings of agonizing shame and painful nakedness as an accompaniment to her genuine expressions of her true self. With the infallibility of a sleepwalker, she will seek out those who, like her parents (though for different reasons), certainly cannot understand her. Because of her blindness caused by repression, she will try to make herself understandable to precisely these people—trying to make possible what cannot be.

During her therapy, Linda, forty-two, fell in love with an older, intelligent, and sensitive man, who nevertheless had to ward off and reject everything—except for eroticism—he could not understand intellectually, including psychotherapy. Yet he was the one to whom she wrote long letters trying to explain the path she had taken in her therapy up to this point. She succeeded in overlooking all signals of his incomprehension and increased her efforts even more, until at last she was forced to recognize that she had again found a father substitute and that this was the reason she had been unable to give up her hopes of at last being understood. This awakening brought her agonizingly sharp feelings of shame, which lasted for a long time.

One day she was able to feel this shame deeply in the session and said: "I feel so ridiculous, as if I've been talking to a wall and expecting it to answer, like a silly child." I asked: "Would you think it ridiculous if you saw a child who had to tell his troubles to a wall because there was no one else available?" The despairing sobbing that followed my question gave Linda access to a part of her former reality that was pervaded by boundless loneliness. It also eventually freed her from her agonizing, self-destructive, repetitive feelings of shame.

Only much later could Linda dare to connect this experience of "a wall" with her own childhood history. For a time this woman, who was normally capable of expressing herself so clearly, described everything in such an extraordinarily complicated way and at such precipitate speed that I couldn't fully understand it. She went through moments of sudden hate and rage, reproaching me for indifference and lack of understanding. Linda could hardly recognize me anymore, although I had not changed. In her estranged feelings she now discovered the estrangement of her mother, who had spent the first year of her life in an orphanage and could not give her daughter any tenderness or closeness. Linda had known that for a long time, but it was only intellectual knowledge. Moreover, compassion for her mother's sad life history had hindered Linda from feeling her own plight; the image of the poor mother had blocked her feelings.

It was not until she could make her reproaches, first toward me and then toward her mother, that the core of her despair became conscious: her lifelong search for closeness and contact that had never been met in infancy and had become repressed. Repressed memories of the shy, distant, absent mother produced in the daughter the feeling of a wall, one that later separated her from other people in such a painful way. She was finally released from a compulsion to repeat that had consisted of constantly seeking a partner who had no understanding of her and then allowing herself to settle into an arrangement where she would feel helplessly dependent on him. The fascination of such tormenting relationships is a result of repressed memories and the struggle for a better outlet at last.

## Perpetuation of Contempt in Perversion and Obsessive Behavior

If we start from the premise that a person's whole development (and his balance, which is based upon it) is dependent on the way *his mother* experienced his *expression of needs and sensations* during his first days and weeks of life, then we must assume that it is here that the *beginning of a later tragedy* might be set. If a mother cannot take pleasure in her child as he is but must have him behave in a particular way, then the first value selection takes place for the child. Now "good" is differentiated from "bad," "nice" from "nasty," and "right" from "wrong." Against this background will follow all his further valuations of himself.

Such an infant must learn that there are things about him for which the mother has "no use." She will expect her child to control his bodily functions as early as possible. On the conscious level his parents apparently want him to do so in order

not to offend against society, but unconsciously they are pro-
tecting their own repression dating from the time when they
were themselves small children afraid of "offending."

Marie Hesse, the mother of the poet and novelist Hermann
Hesse, described in her diaries how her own will was broken at
the age of four. When her son was four years old, she suffered
greatly under his defiant behavior and battled against it with
varying degrees of success. At the age of fifteen, Hermann
Hesse was sent to an institution for the care of epileptics and
defectives in Stetten, "to put an end to his defiance once and
for all." In an affecting and angry letter from Stetten, Hesse
wrote to his parents: "If I were a bigot, and not a human being,
I could perhaps hope for your understanding." All the same,
his release from the home was made conditional upon his
"improvement," and so the boy "improved."

In a later poem dedicated to his parents, denial and idealization are restored: he reproaches *himself* that it had been "his
character" that had made life so difficult for his parents. Many
people suffer all their lives from this oppressive feeling of guilt,
the sense of not having lived up to their parents' expectations.
This feeling is stronger than any intellectual insight they
might have, that it is not a child's task or duty to satisfy his
parent's needs. No argument can overcome these guilt feelings,
for they have their beginnings in life's earliest period, and from
that they derive their intensity and obduracy. They can be
resolved only slowly, with the help of the Four Steps.

Probably the greatest of wounds—not to have been loved
just as one truly was—cannot heal without the work of mourning. It can be either more or less successfully resisted and covered up (as in grandiosity and depression), or constantly torn
open again in the compulsion to repeat. We encounter this latter possibility in obsessive behavior and in perversion, where
the mother's (or father's) scornful reactions to the child's behav-

ior have stayed with him as repressed memory, stored up in his body. (The same happens with mistreatments and molestations that have been endured.) The mother often reacted with surprise and horror, aversion and disgust, shock and indignation, or fear and panic to the child's most natural impulses—his autoerotic behavior, investigation and discovery of his own body, urination and defecation, or his curiosity or rage in response to betrayal and injustice. Later, all these experiences remain closely linked with the mother's horrified eyes. They drive the former child to obsessions and perversions in which the traumatic scenes that were endured can be reproduced. In order for pain to be avoided, the true meaning of these scenes must remain unrecognizable to the person himself.

The patient goes through torment when he reveals to the therapist his hitherto secret sexual and autoerotic behavior. He may, of course, also relate this material quite unemotionally, merely giving information, as if speaking of some other person. Such a report, however, will neither help him break out of his loneliness nor lead him back to the reality of his childhood. It is only when he is willing not to fend off his feelings of shame and fear, but rather to accept and experience them, that he can discover the real past reasons for these feelings. His most harmless behavior will then cause him to feel mean, dirty, or completely annihilated. He is surprised indeed when he realizes how long this repressed feeling of shame has survived, and how it has found a place alongside his tolerant and advanced views of sexuality. These experiences first show the person that his early adaptation by means of splitting was not an expression of cowardice, but that it was really his only chance to survive, to escape his fear of annihilation.

Can a mother be so menacing? Yes, if she was always proud of being her mother's dear, good daughter, who was dry at the age of six months and clean at a year, who at three could "mother" her younger siblings, and so forth.* In her own baby, such a mother sees the split-off and never-experienced part of her self, of whose breakthrough into consciousness she is afraid. She also sees the uninhibited sibling baby, whom she mothered at such an early age and only now envies and perhaps hates in the person of her own child. So she trains her child with looks, despite what may be a greater intellectual wisdom than her own mother's.

As the child grows up, he cannot cease living his own truth and expressing it somewhere, perhaps in complete secrecy. In this way a person can have adapted completely to the demands of his surroundings and can have developed a false self, but in his perversion or his obsessions he still allows a portion of his true self to survive—in torment. And so the true self lives on, but underground, in the same conditions as the child once did with his disgusted mother, whose memory in the meantime he has repressed. In his perversion and obsessions he constantly reenacts the same drama: A horrified mother is necessary before sexual satisfaction is possible; orgasm (for instance, with a fetish) can be achieved only in a climate of self-contempt; criticism can be expressed only in (seemingly) absurd, unaccountable, and frightening obsessive fantasies. Nothing will better serve to acquaint us with the hidden tragedy of certain unconscious mother-child relationships than witnessing the destructive power of the compulsion to repeat, and that compulsion's dumb, unconscious communication in the shaping of its drama.

It is of primary importance that, although the patient may *experience* the therapist as hostile to his desires and compulsions,

---

*This particular form of tampering with a child's natural development may not be as familiar to readers in the United States as it is in Europe. Many of my patients were dry at five months, and their mothers were quite proud of this "achievement." American readers may be better acquainted with such practices as scheduled feedings and training infants to sleep through the night by ignoring their cries.

critical and contemptuous, the therapist should never in fact really be so. This may sound obvious, but it is not always true in practice. In fact, the therapist sometimes does just the opposite, quite unconsciously. Because he fears his own repressed terror, he may be unable to bear being turned into a hostile figure and may demonstrate his tolerance in a way that does not allow the child's fear and confusion to come up in the patient.

Such a therapist may emphasize that his patients are for him *always* adult clients and not "children"—as if the feelings of a child were something to be ashamed of, and not something valuable and helpful. Occasionally one hears similar remarks about sickness, when a therapist is eager to consider his patients as healthy as possible; he may warn them against "dangerous regression," as if "sickness" were not sometimes the only possible way of expressing the person's plight. Many people have, after all, been trying all their lives to be as adult and healthy (normal) as possible. They should be given support for the relief they feel at the discovery of this socially conditioned straitjacket of child-rejection and "normalcy-worship" within themselves. By giving it up they will get in touch with their true feelings. This is one of the reasons I prefer to use the word "patient" instead of "client," which is more frequently used by therapists today. It was not until I experienced myself as a patient, as a suffering person, that I could find my way out of the trap of repression and help myself. As the "client" of (seemingly) "good therapists," I could find only *their* knowledge, something which was of no help at all in my quest for healing.

Mark, thirty-two, who suffered under his perversion and constantly feared the rejection of others, bore within himself the unconscious memory of his mother's rejection. Without knowing why, he was compelled to do things that his social circle and society in general disapprove of and despise, although he feared the punishment he was provoking. If society were suddenly to have honored his form of perversion (as happens in certain circles), he would perhaps have had to change his compulsion, but that would never have freed him. What he was compelled to seek was not permission to use one or another fetish, but—with the hope for a better outcome—his mother's disgusted and horrified eyes. He looked for this response in his therapist, too, using all possible means to provoke him to disgust, horror, and aversion. This provocation of course recounted what had actually happened at the beginning of Mark's life. This recounting was of no use to him, however, as long as the old feelings were blocked. The most brilliant intellect cannot break this block down. But with the help of the Four Steps—with his complaints (in Step 1), with the experience of profound feelings (in Step 2), with confronting the abuses and condemning the deeds (in Step 3)—he could give up his acting out. Thanks to Step 4, he now knew what he *really* needed.

If a person can see through to the goals and compulsions behind this sort of provocation, then the whole decayed building collapses and gives way to true, deep, and defenseless mourning. When this happens, all the distortions are no longer necessary. This is a clear demonstration of how mistaken the attempt is to show a patient his "sexual conflicts" if he has been trained from earliest childhood on to *feel nothing.* How can these conflicts be experienced without feelings of rage, abandonment, jealousy, loneliness, love?

In the last ten years I have received many letters from readers who wrote to me to say that as teenagers they had been sexually abused, seduced, and emotionally exploited by adult men, without ever being able to recognize this fact because of their blindness stemming from repressed childhood memories. It was not before they read my book *Thou Shalt Not Be Aware* that they began to have doubts and suspicions. For the first time in their lives, they dared to question the behavior of their perpetrators. The idea that they had been betrayed, that their longing for love and affection had been exploited, never before occurred to them, because they were unable to feel. The only path available to them was to idealize the seducer, the big friend, savior, teacher, master, and to become addicted to a special form of sexual behavior, or to drugs, or to both. Struggling for social acceptance of special forms of addictions, sexual and nonsexual, is one of the many ways to avoid confrontation with our own history.

There are many people whose needs for protection, care, and tenderness, whose unmet longing for love, were very early sexualized and who lived their lives with various sexual fixations without ever having faced their history. They join groups, accept uncritically theories that confirm their fixations, and pretend to share with others "scientific" knowledge, while they unconsciously disguise their own repressed history. As long as they do, they damage others in the same way they have been damaged, without any remorse.

I think that the future (the therapy) of these people and their victims is jeopardized by every kind of ideology. They should rather be informed that it is possible to discover one's history, to work it through, and to liberate oneself from fixations that can be destructive for oneself and others. It is very striking to see how often a sexual "addiction" ceases when the patient begins to experience *his own* feelings and can recognize his *true* needs.

The following quote is taken from a report about St. Pauli, Hamburg's red-light district, that appeared in the German magazine *Stern* (June 8, 1978): "You experience the masculine dream, as seductive as it is absurd, of being coddled by women like a baby and at the same time commanding them like a pascha." This "dream" is in fact not absurd; it arises from the infant's most genuine and legitimate needs. Our world would be very different if the majority of babies had the chance to rule over their mothers like paschas and to be coddled by them, without having to concern themselves with their mothers' needs.

The reporter asked some of the regular clients what gave them most pleasure in these establishments and summarized their answers as follows:

> that the girls are available and completely at the customer's disposal; they do *not require protestations of love like girlfriends.* There are *no obligations, psychological dramas,* or *pangs of conscience* when desire has passed: "You pay and are free!" Even (and especially) the *humiliation* that such an encounter also involves for the client can *increase stimulation*—but that is less willingly mentioned.[*]

The humiliation, self-disgust, and self-contempt trigger the past situation and, through the compulsion to repeat, produce the same tragic conditions for pleasure. Seen in this way, the compulsion to repeat is a great opportunity. It can be resolved when the feelings in the present situation can be felt and clarified through the Four Steps. If no use is made of this opportunity, if its message is ignored, the compulsion to repeat will continue without abating for the person's entire lifetime, although its form may change.

What is unconscious cannot be abolished by proclamation or prohibition. One can, however, develop sensitivity toward recognizing it and begin to experience it consciously, and thus eventually gain control over it. A mother cannot truly respect her child as long as she does not realize what deep shame she

---

[*]Italics added.

causes him with an ironic remark, intended only to cover her own uncertainty. Indeed, she cannot be aware of how deeply humiliated, despised, and devalued her child feels, if she herself has never consciously suffered these feelings, and if she tries to fend them off with irony.

The same can be said for most psychiatrists, clinical psychologists, and therapists. Certainly, they do not use words like "bad," "dirty," "naughty," "egoistic," "rotten"—but among themselves they sometimes speak of "narcissistic," "exhibitionistic," "destructive," "regressive," or "borderline" patients without noticing that they give these words a pejorative meaning. It may be that their abstract vocabulary, their supposedly objective attitudes, even the way they formulate their theories and zealously make their diagnoses, all have something in common with a mother's contemptuous looks—which they could, if they were willing, trace to the accommodating three-year-old girl or boy within themselves.

It is understandable that a patient's scornful attitude could induce a therapist to protect his superiority with the help of theory. But if he builds such a wall, the patient's true self will not be visible to him. It will hide from him just as it did from the mother's disgusted eyes. We could, however, make good use of our sensitivity by instead detecting pieces of the story of a despised child that lie behind all the patient's expressions of contempt. When the therapist's resources are used in this way, it is easier for him not to feel he is being attacked and to drop his need to hide behind his theories. Knowledge of theory is essential, but knowledge of the *right* theory has no defensive function: It is no longer the successor of a strict, controlling mother, forcing the therapist to accommodate himself to it.

## "DEPRAVITY" AS "EVIL" IN
## HERMANN HESSE'S CHILDHOOD WORLD

It is very difficult to describe how people deal with the contempt under which they suffered as children—especially the contempt for all their sensual enjoyment and pleasure in living—without giving concrete examples. With the aid of theoretical models, I could certainly describe the various defense mechanisms, especially the defense against feelings, but doing so would fail to communicate the emotional climate, which alone evokes a person's suffering and so makes identification and empathy possible for the reader. With purely theoretical representations we therapists remain "outside"; from there we can talk about the "others," classify, group, and label them by making diagnoses, and discuss them in a language only we understand. As I refuse to do all that, I need to use examples. It is only through the details of a specific life that we can show how a person has experienced the naughtiness of his childhood as "wickedness itself." Only the history of an individual life can make us realize how impossible it is for a child to recognize his parents' compulsions as such and to realize that this blindness can persist throughout the adult's whole life, try as he may to break out of his inner prison.

I use the example of the poet and novelist Hermann Hesse to demonstrate this very complicated situation. This example has the advantage of having been published, and published by the person himself, so that the connections that I postulate can be clarified with concrete examples from his life.

At the beginning of his novel *Demian,* Hermann Hesse describes the "goodness and purity" of a parental home in which there is no room for a child's fibs. (It is not difficult to recognize the author's own parental home in this novel, and he confirms this indirectly.) The child is alone with his sin and feels that he is depraved, wicked, and outcast, though nobody scolds him, since no one as yet knows the "terrible facts." This situation is of course a common one in real life, and Hesse's idealized way of describing such a "pure" household is not strange to us either. It reflects both the child's point of view and the hidden cruelty of commonplace methods, with which we are only too familiar, used to teach moral "values."

> Like most parents [writes Hesse], mine were no help with the new problems of puberty, to which no reference was ever made. All they did was take *endless trouble* in supporting my hopeless attempts to *deny reality* and to continue dwelling in a childhood world that was becoming *more and more unreal*. I have no idea whether parents can be of help, and I do not blame mine. It was my own affair to come to terms with myself and to find my own way, and like most well-brought-up children, I managed it badly. (p. 49)*

A child's parents seem to him to be free of sexual desires, for they have means and possibilities of hiding their sexual activities, whereas the child is always under surveillance.† The first part of *Demian,* it seems to me, is very evocative and easy to appreciate, even for people from quite different milieus. What makes the later parts of the novel so peculiarly difficult must in some way be related to Hesse's parents' and grandparents' moral values (they were missionary families). These permeate many of

---

*Italics added.

†In his story "A Child's Heart," Hesse writes: "The adults acted as if the world were perfect and as if they themselves were demigods, we children were nothing but scum. . . . Again and again, after a few days, even after a few hours, something happened that should not have been allowed, something wretched, depressing, and shaming. Again and again, in the midst of the noblest and staunchest decisions and vows, I fell abruptly, inescapably, into sin and wickedness, into ordinary bad habits. Why was it this way?" (pp. 7, 8)

his stories but can perhaps be most easily sensed in *Demian*.

Although Sinclair, the hero, has already had his own experience of cruelty (blackmail by an older boy), it has given him no key to a better understanding of the world. "Wickedness" for him is "depravity" (here is the missionaries' language): it is neither hate nor cruelty, but such trivialities as drinking in a tavern.

As a little boy, Hermann Hesse took over from his parents this particular concept of wickedness as depravity. It is like a foreign body that he seeks to locate and uproot from his personality. This is why everything that happens in *Demian* after the appearance of the god Abraxas, who is to "unite the godly and the devilish," is so curiously removed. Wickedness is supposed to be artfully united with goodness here, but we are not touched by it. One has the impression that, for the boy, this is something strange, threatening, and above all unknown, from which he nevertheless cannot free himself. His emotional belief in "depravity" is already joined to fear and guilt:

> Once more I was trying most strenuously to construct an intimate "world of light" for myself out of the shambles of a period of devastation; once more I sacrificed everything within me to the aim of banishing darkness and evil from myself. (pp. 81–82)

In the Zürich exhibition (1977) to commemorate the centennial of Hesse's birth, a picture was displayed that had hung above the little Hermann's bed and that he had grown up with. In this picture, on the right, we see the "good" road to heaven, full of thorns, difficulties, and suffering. On the left, we see the easy, pleasurable road that inevitably leads to hell. Taverns play a prominent part on this road, probably because devout women hoped to keep their husbands and sons away from these wicked places with this threatening representation.

These taverns play an important role in *Demian*—ironically so, because Hesse had no urge at all to get drunk in such taverns, though he certainly did wish to break out of the narrowness of his parents' values.

Every child forms his first image of what is "bad" quite concretely, by what is forbidden—by his parents' prohibitions, taboos, and fears. He will have a long way to go before he can free himself from these parental values and see without filters what he has believed to be "badness" in himself. He will then no longer regard it as "depraved" and "wicked," but as a comprehensible latent reaction to injuries he had to repress when a child. As an adult, he can discover the causes and free himself from this unconscious reaction. He also has the opportunity to apologize for what he has done to others out of ignorance, blindness, and confusion, and doing so will help him to avoid repetitions of acts he no longer wishes to continue.

Unfortunately, the path to clarification was not open to Hermann Hesse. The following passage from *Demian* shows how deeply the perceived loss of his parents' love threatened his search for his true self:

> But where we have given of our love and respect not from habit but of our own free will, where we have been disciples and friends out of our inmost hearts, it is a bitter and horrible moment when we suddenly recognize that the current within us wants to pull us away from what is dearest to us. Then every thought that rejects the friend and mentor turns on our own hearts like a *poisoned barb,* then each blow struck in defense *flies back into one's own face,* the words "disloyalty" and "ingratitude" strike the person who feels he was morally sound *like catcalls and stigma,* and the *frightened heart flees timidly back* to the *charmed valleys of childhood* virtues, unable to believe that this break, too, must be made, this bond also broken. (p. 127)*

---

*Italics added.

And in his story "A Child's Heart" we read:

> If I were to reduce all my feelings and their painful conflicts
> to a single name, I can think of no other word but: dread. It
> was dread, dread and uncertainty, that I felt in all those hours
> of shattered childhood felicity: dread of punishment, dread of
> my own conscience, dread of stirrings in my soul which I con-
> sidered forbidden and criminal. (p. 10)

In this story Hesse portrays with great tenderness and
understanding the feelings of an eleven-year-old boy who
has stolen some dried figs from his beloved father's room so
that he could have in his possession something that belongs
to his father. Guilt feelings, fear, and despair torment him
in his loneliness and are replaced at last by the deepest
humiliation and shame when his "wicked deed" is discovered. The strength of this portrayal leads us to surmise that
it concerns a real episode from Hesse's own childhood. This
surmise becomes certainty, thanks to a note made by his
mother on November 11, 1889: "Hermann's theft of figs
discovered."

From the entries in his mother's diary and from the exten-
sive exchange of letters between both parents and various
members of the family, which have been available since 1966,
it is possible to guess at the small boy's painful path. Hesse,
like so many gifted children, was so difficult for his parents to
bear not despite but *because of* his inner riches. Often a child's
very gifts (his great intensity of feeling, depth of experience,
curiosity, intelligence, quickness—and his ability to be critical) will confront his parents with conflicts that they have
long sought to keep at bay by means of rules and regulations.
These regulations must then be rescued at the cost of the
child's development. All this can lead to an apparently para-

doxical situation when parents who are proud of their gifted child and who even admire him are forced by their own repression to reject, suppress, or even destroy what is *best,* because truest, in that child. Two of Hesse's mother's observations may illustrate how this work of destruction can be combined with apparent loving care:

1. (1881): "Hermann is going to nursery school, his violent temperament causes us much distress." (1966, p. 10) The child was three years old.

2. (1884): "Things are going better with Hermann, whose education causes us so much distress and trouble. From the 21st of January to the 5th of June he lived wholly in the boys' house and only spent Sundays with us. He behaved well there but came home pale, thin and *depressed.* The *effects are decidedly good and salutary.* He is much *easier to manage now.*" (1966, pp. 13–14) The child now was seven years old.*

On November 14, 1883, his father, Johannes Hesse, wrote:

Hermann, who was considered almost a model of good behavior in the boys' house is sometimes *hardly to be borne.* Though it would be very humiliating *for us*[!], I am earnestly considering whether we should not place him in an *institution* or *another household.* We are too nervous and weak for him, and the whole household [is] too undisciplined and irregular. He seems to be gifted for everything: he observes the moon and the clouds, extemporizes for long periods on the harmonium, draws wonderful pictures with pencil or pen, can sing quite well when he wants to, and is never at a loss for a rhyme.†
(1966, p. 13)

*Italics added.

†Italics added.

In the strongly idealized picture of his childhood and his parents that we encounter in *Hermann Lauscher,** Hesse has completely abandoned the original, rebellious, "difficult," and—for his parents—troublesome child he once was. He had no way to accommodate this important part of his self and so was forced to expel it. Perhaps this is why his great and genuine longing for his true self remained unfulfilled.

That Hermann Hesse was not deficient in courage, talent, or depth of feeling is, of course, evident in his works and in many of his letters, especially the outraged letter from the institution in Stetten. But his father's answer to this letter (see Hesse 1966), his mother's notes, and the passages from *Demian* and "A Child's Heart" quoted above show us clearly how the crushing weight of the denial of his childhood pain pressed on him. Despite his enormous acclaim and success, and despite the Nobel Prize, Hesse in his mature years suffered from the tragic and painful state of being separated from his true self, to which doctors refer offhandedly as depression.

## THE MOTHER AS SOCIETY'S AGENT DURING THE FIRST YEARS OF LIFE

If we were to tell a patient that in other societies his perversion would not be a problem, that it is a problem here only because

---

*"When my childhood at times stirs my heart, it is like a gold-framed, deep-toned picture in which predominates a wealth of chestnuts and alders, an indescribably delightful morning light and a background of splendid mountains. All the hours in my life, in which I was allowed a short period of peace, forgetful of the world; all the lonely walks, which I took over beautiful mountains; all the moments in which an unexpected happiness, or love without desire, carried me away from yesterday and tomorrow; all these can be given no more precious name than when I compare them with this green picture of my earliest life." (*Gesammelte Werke,* vol. I, Frankfurt: M. Suhrkamp, 1970, p. 218)

it is our society that is sick and produces constrictions and constraints, we would certainly be telling him at least a partial
truth, but it would be of little help to him. He would feel,
rather, that as an individual, with his own individual history,
he was being passed over and misunderstood, for this interpretation makes too little of his own very real tragedy. What he
most needs to understand is his compulsion to repeat, and the
state of affairs behind it to which this compulsion bears witness. His plight is no doubt the result of social pressures, but
these do not have their effect on his psyche through abstract
knowledge; they are firmly anchored in his earliest affective
experience with his mother. Thus his problems cannot be
solved with *words,* but only through *experience*—not merely cor-
rective experience as an adult but, above all, through a conscious experience of his early fear of his beloved mother's contempt and his subsequent feelings of indignation and sadness.
Mere words, however skilled the interpretation, will leave
unchanged or even deepened the split between intellectual
speculation and the knowledge of the body, the split from
which he already suffers.

One can therefore hardly free an addict from the cruelty of
his addiction by showing him how the absurdity, exploitation,
and perversity of society cause our neuroses and perversions,
however true this may be. The addict will love such explanations and eagerly believe them, because they spare him the pain
of the truth. But things we can see through do not make us
sick, although they may arouse our indignation, anger, sadness,
or feelings of impotence. What makes us sick are those things
we cannot see through, society's constraints that we have
absorbed through our mother's eyes. No amount of reading or
learning can free us from those eyes and the repressed memories of our parents' obsessions and other symptoms, which
found expression in the mistreatment of their children.

To put it another way: Many people suffering from severe symptoms are very intelligent. They read in newspapers and books about the absurdity of the arms race, about exploitation through capitalism, diplomatic insincerity, the arrogance and manipulation of power, submission of the weak, and the impotence of individuals—and they have given thought to these subjects. What they do not see, because they cannot see them, are the absurdities enacted by their own mothers when they were still tiny children. They cannot remember what their parents' attitudes were back then, because they were forced to suppress their rage and pain. When this early experience can be recalled, parental constraints are more easily disclosed.

Oppression and the forcing of submission do not begin in the office, factory, or political party; they begin in the very first weeks of an infant's life. Afterward they are repressed and are then, because of their very nature, inaccessible to argument. Nothing changes in the character of submission or dependency, when it is only their object that is changed.

Political action can be fed by the unconscious rage of children who have been misused, imprisoned, exploited, cramped, and drilled. This rage can be partially discharged in fighting "enemies," without having to give up the idealization of one's own parents. The old dependency will then simply be shifted to a new group or leader. If, however, disillusionment and the resultant mourning can be lived through, social and political disengagement do not usually follow, but our actions are freed from the compulsion to repeat. They can then have a clear goal, formed out of conscious decisions.

Once our own reality has been faced and experienced, the inner necessity to keep building up new illusions and denials in order to avoid the experience of that reality disappears. We then realize that all our lives we have feared and struggled to ward off something that really cannot happen any longer; it has already happened, happened at the very beginning of our lives while we were completely dependent.

Therapeutic effects (in the form of temporary improvement) may be achieved if a strict conscience can be replaced by the therapist's or the group's more tolerant one. The aim of therapy, however, is not to correct the past, but to enable the patient both to confront his own history and to grieve over it. The patient has to discover early memories within himself and must become consciously aware of his parents' unconscious manipulation and contempt, so that he can free himself from them. As long as he has to make do with a substitute tolerance, borrowed from his therapist or his group, the contemptuous attitudes he inherited from his parents will remain hidden in his unconscious, unchanged despite all his improved intellectual knowledge and intentions. This contemptuous attitude will show itself in the patient's human relationships and will continue to torment him as long as it functions in the cells of his body. The contents of the unconscious remain unchanged and timeless. It is only as these contents become conscious that change can begin.

## THE LONELINESS OF THE CONTEMPTUOUS

The contempt shown by many disturbed people may have various forerunners in their life history, but the function all expressions of contempt have in common is the defense against unwanted feelings. Contempt simply evaporates, having lost its point, when it is no longer useful as a shield—against the child's shame over his desperate, unreturned love; against his feeling of inadequacy; or above all against his rage that his parents were not available. Once we are able to feel and understand the repressed emotions of childhood, we will no longer need contempt as a defense against them. On the other hand, as long as we despise the other person and overvalue our own achievements ("he can't do what I can do"), we do not have to mourn the fact that love is not forthcoming without achievement. Nevertheless, if we avoid this mourning it means that we remain at bottom the one who is despised, for we have to despise everything in ourselves that is not wonderful, good, and clever. Thus we perpetuate the loneliness of childhood: We despise weakness, helplessness, uncertainty—in short, the child in ourselves and in others.

The contempt for others in grandiose, successful people always includes disrespect for their own true selves, as their scorn implies: "Without these superior qualities of mine, a person is completely worthless." This means further: "Without these achievements, these gifts, I could never be loved, would never have been loved." Grandiosity in the adult guarantees that the illusion continues: "I was loved." The way out of this confusing and stressful self-betrayal may well be illustrated by John's dream.

John, forty-eight, who came back to therapy because of tormenting obsessions, repeatedly dreamed that he was on a lookout tower that stood in a swampy area at the edge of a town dear to him. In reality, the town had no such tower, but it belonged unequivocally to John's dream landscape, and he knew it well. From there he had a lovely view, but he felt sad and deserted. There was an elevator in the tower, and in the dream there were all kinds of difficulties over entrance tickets and obstacles on the way to this tower. The dream recurred often, with the same feelings of being deserted.

Only after much had changed in the course of therapy were there new variations in the dream, too, and at last it changed in a decisive way. John was first surprised to dream that he already had entrance tickets, but the tower had been demolished and there was no longer a view. Instead, he saw a bridge that joined the swampy district to the town. He could thus go on foot into the town and see "not everything" but "some things close up." John, who suffered from an elevator phobia, was somewhat relieved, for he had felt considerable anxiety riding in this elevator. Speaking of the dream, he said he was perhaps no longer dependent on always having a complete view, on always seeing everything—being on top and cleverer than other people. He now could go on foot like everyone else.

John was the more astonished when he later dreamed that he was suddenly sitting in this elevator in the tower again and was being drawn upward as in a chair lift, without feeling any fear. He enjoyed the ride, got out at the top, and, strange to say, found colorful life all about him. He was on a plateau, from where he had a view of the valleys. There was also a town up there, with a bazaar full of colorful wares; a school where children were practicing ballet and he could join in (this had been a childhood wish); and groups of people holding discussions, with whom he sat and talked. He felt integrated into this society, just as he was. Although the dream expressed his wishes rather than reality, it showed him his true, *real* needs: to be loved and to love beyond his achievements. This dream impressed him deeply. He said:

My earlier dreams of the tower showed my isolation and loneliness. At home, as the eldest, I was always ahead of my siblings, my parents could not match my intelligence, and in all intellectual matters I was alone. On the one hand, I had to demonstrate my knowledge in order to be taken seriously, and on the other, I had to hide it or my parents would say: "Your studies are going to your head! Do you think you are better than everyone else, just because you had the chance to study? Without your mother's sacrifice and your father's hard work you would never have been able to do it." That made me feel guilty and I tried to hide my difference, my interests, and my gifts. I wanted to be like the others. There was no way for me to be true to myself, to respect me as I really was.

So John had searched for his tower and had struggled with obstacles (on the way, with entrance tickets, his fears, and more), and when he got to the top—that is, was smarter than the others—he felt lonely and deserted.

It is a well-known and common paradox that parents who take up this grudging and competitive attitude toward their child at the same time urge him on to the greatest achievement and are proud of his success. Thus John *had to* look for his tower and had to encounter obstacles, as well. Eventually he went through a revolt against this pressure toward achievement and stress, and so the tower disappeared in the first of the dreams I have described here. He could give up his grandiose fantasy of seeing *everything* from above and could look at things in his beloved town (in himself) from close by.

Only now did it become clear to him that he had felt compelled to isolate himself from others by means of his contempt and at the same time was isolated and separated from his true self—at least from its helpless, uncertain part.

Contempt as a rule will cease with the beginning of mourning for the irreversible that cannot be changed, for contempt, too, has in its own way served to deny the reality of the past. It is, after all, less painful to think that the others do not understand because they are too stupid. Then one can make efforts to explain things to them, and the illusion of being understood ("if only I can express myself properly") can be maintained.* If, however,

---

*Devastating examples of this process are the works of van Gogh (see Nagara 1967), who so wonderfully and so unsuccessfully courted the favor of his mother with all the means at his disposal.

this effort is relaxed, one is forced to realize that understanding was not possible, since the repression of the parents' own childhood needs made them blind to their children's needs.

Even alert parents cannot always understand their children, but they will respect their children's feelings even when they cannot understand them. Where there is no such respect, their children seek refuge from a painful truth in ideologies. Nationalism, racism, and fascism are in fact nothing other than ideological guises of the flight from painful, unconscious memories of endured contempt into the dangerous, destructive disrespect for human life, glorified as a political program. The formerly hidden cruelty that was exercised upon the powerless child now becomes only too apparent in the violence of such "political" groups. Its origins in childhood, in the total disregard of the former child, however, remain concealed or absolutely denied, not only by the members of these groups but by society as a whole.

## ACHIEVING FREEDOM FROM CONTEMPT AND RESPECTING LIFE

Sexual perversions, obsessions, and flights into ideologies are not the only possibilities for perpetuating the tragedy of early suffering from contempt. There are countless ways we may transmit the family climate under which we suffered as children. There are people, for example, who never say a loud or angry word, who seem to be only good and noble, and who still give others the palpable feeling of being ridiculous or stupid or too noisy, or at any rate too common compared with themselves. They do not know it and perhaps do not intend it, but this is what they radiate: the attitude of their parents, of which they have never been aware. The children of such persons find it particularly difficult to formulate any reproach until they learn to do so in their therapy.

Then there are the people who can seem very friendly, if a shade patronizing, but in whose presence one feels as if one were nothing. They convey the feeling that they are the only ones who exist, the only ones who have anything interesting or relevant to say. The others can only stand there and admire them in fascination, or turn away in disappointment and sorrow about their own lack of worth, unable to express themselves in these persons' presence. These people might be the children of grandiose parents, whom they as children had no hope of emulating; but later, as adults, they unconsciously pass on this atmosphere to those around them.

Quite a different impression will be given by those people who, as children, were intellectually far beyond their parents and therefore admired by them, but who also therefore had to solve their own problems alone. These people, who give us a feeling of their intellectual strength and will power, also seem to demand that we, too, ought to fight off any feeling of weakness with intellectual means. In their presence one feels one can't be recognized as a person with problems—just as they and their problems were unrecognized by their parents, for whom they always had to be strong.

Keeping these examples in mind, it is easy to see why some professors or writers who are quite capable of expressing themselves clearly will use language that is so convoluted and arcane that their students or readers must struggle angrily to acquire ideas that they then can make little use of. The students may well experience feelings similar to those their teacher was once forced to suppress in relation to his parents. If the students themselves become teachers one day, they will then have the opportunity to hand on this unusable knowledge like a priceless jewel (because it has cost them so much).

It greatly aids the success of therapeutic work when we become aware of our parents' destructive patterns at work within us. But to free ourselves from these patterns we need more than an intellectual awareness: we need an emotional confrontation with our parents in an inner dialogue. With the Four-Step Method, we resolve *parts* of our confusion in each single confrontation.

When the patient has emotionally worked through the history of her childhood and has thus regained her sense of being alive, the goal of therapy has been reached. She will then be able to use the tools she has learned whenever feelings from her past are triggered by present events. As time goes on, she will use them more and more effectively and will need less time for this work. The "map" of her life will be available for her whenever she needs it.

The therapist must leave it up to the patient to decide whether she will take a regular job or not; whether she wants to live alone or with a partner; whether she wants to join a political party, and if so, which one. All of these decisions must be her own. Her life story, her experiences, and what she has learned from them will all play a role in how she will live. It is not the task of the therapist to "socialize" her, or to "raise her consciousness" (not even politically, for every form of indoctrination denies her autonomy), or to "make friendships possible for her." All that is her own affair.

When the patient has consciously and repeatedly experienced how the whole process of her upbringing manipulated and damaged her in her childhood, and with what desires for revenge this has left her, then she will see through manipulation more quickly than before and will herself have less need to manipulate others. Such a patient will be able to join groups if she wishes without again becoming helplessly dependent or bound, for she has consciously gone through the helplessness and dependency of her childhood. She will be in less danger of idealizing people or systems if she has realized clearly how as a child she took every word uttered by her mother or father for the deepest wisdom. She may momentarily experience, while listening to a lecture or reading a book, the same old childish fascination and admiration, but she will sooner recognize and reject the underlying emptiness that lurks behind these manipulative and seductive words. A person who has matured through her own experience cannot be tricked with fascinating, incomprehensible words. Finally, a person who has consciously worked through the whole tragedy of her own fate will recognize another's suffering more clearly, though the other may be trying to hide it. She will not be scornful of others' feelings, whatever their nature, because she takes her own feelings seriously and knows how to work with them. She surely will not keep the vicious circle of contempt turning.

This achievement will have not only personal consequences for the individual and her family, but also far-reaching significance for society as a whole. People who discover their past with the help of their feelings, who learn through therapy to clarify these feelings, to look for their *real causes,* and to resolve the transference, will no longer be compelled to displace their hatred onto innocents in order to protect those who have in fact earned this hatred. They will be capable of hating what is hateful and of loving what deserves love. Once they dare to see who brought them to their plight and how it was done, they will be better oriented in present reality and able to avoid acting blindly, unconsciously. They will no longer behave like the mistreated children they were, children who must protect their parents and who therefore need a scapegoat for the buried emotions that torment them.

The future of democracy and democratic freedom depends on our capacity to take this very step and to recognize that it is simply impossible to struggle successfully against hatred out-side ourselves, while ignoring its messages within. We must know and use the tools that are necessary to resolve it: We must feel and understand its source and its legitimacy. There is no point in appealing to our goodwill, our kindness, and a common spirit of love, as long as the path to clarifying our feelings is blocked by the unconscious fear of our parents. This fear can be disguised by any number of political or religious ideologies, as well as by high-sounding and seemingly virtuous moral judgments.

*Consciously experiencing our legitimate hatred is liberating,* not just because of the discharge of long-held tensions in the body but above all because it opens our eyes to reality (both past and present) and frees us of lies and illusions. It gives us back repressed memories and helps dispel attendant symptoms. It is therefore empowering without being destructive. Repressed hatred can be resolved as soon as it is felt, understood, and rec-ognized as legitimate. It can then arise again, appropriately and consciously, when prompted by new causes: We will have a new capacity to identify cruelty and injustice, and to speak out and fight against it.

*But illegitimate hatred never disappears.* It may switch scape-goats, but it will remain ever-present and undiluted. It cannot be appeased: It poisons and blinds the soul, devours the mem-ory and the mind, and kills the capacity for compassion and insight. Its destructive power stems from a history of horror that has been repressed and stored in the body but that, with-out effective therapy, has no direct access to the conscious mind. Hating and offending an innocent person, using him as a scapegoat, can only strengthen the walls of our inner prison of confusion, isolation, fear, and loneliness; it cannot free us. A house built out of self-betrayal will sooner or later fall down and mercilessly destroy human life—if not that of the builder, then that of his children, who will sense the lie without being aware of it and who will end up paying the full price for this hidden arrangement.

A person who can honestly and without self-deception deal with his hatred and other "negative" (unwanted) feelings has no need to disguise them with the help of ideologies. The basic similarity of the various nationalistic movements flourishing today reveals that their motives have nothing to do with the real interests of the people who are fighting and hating but instead have very much to do with those people's childhood histories. The mistreatment, humiliation, and exploitation of children is the same worldwide, as is the means of avoiding the memory of it. Individuals who do not want to know their own truth collude in denial with society as a whole, looking for a common "enemy" on whom to act out their repressed rage. But as the inhabitants of this shrinking planet near the end of the twentieth century, the danger inherent in self-deception is growing exponentially—and we can afford it less than ever. Fortunately, at the same time, we now have the tools we need to truly understand ourselves, as we were and as we are. People who are willing to delve inside themselves for their personal history will become capable, through their fully awakened consciousness, of shedding light—more light than has ever before been possible—into the murky darkness that permeates our political and social activities, as well as our personal lives.

# *Afterword*

Dear Reader,

This letter is addressed to you in a very personal sense. It is addressed to the true self within you, who has lost the way or is on the point of giving up but is beginning to realize it and feels the pain. Perhaps you had to leave that true self far behind, as old fears made you take refuge beneath the many masks, roles, and pretenses that have helped you conceal that pain from yourself, or as you sought to deny the person you really are—and have a right to be—through work, achievement, or worldly success. But the gates to that self are not yet completely shut. As long as there is breath in your body, you can still throw them open and find yourself. This is, above all, what I want to say to you. I myself did not know it for a long time and have gained greatly from this knowledge.

It was principally for this reason that I decided to share what information and advice I could in this revised version of the

*Drama,* realizing at the same time that to do the job as extensively as I'd like, I would have to write an entirely new book. I wanted to relate my personal experiences with Stettbacher's Four-Step Method of therapy, but as there was not room here to do so, I will be writing another book, one in which I will be able to describe what I learned in the course of self-therapy so that you can see how it may be of use to you. There are, however, important things that I had to say in this book, and not elsewhere.

As I wrote the new Introduction to this book, I found myself thinking of the letters I receive from people who have read the *Drama.* The readers often have described how their long-withheld emotions were awakened, but how they then found themselves at a loss to find a way to work with these feelings in order to free themselves from the consequences of childhood damage. To finally be able to feel and cry (the second step in the Four-Step Method) is without a doubt a relief. But simply opening old wounds without understanding how to proceed can be very frightening. Although feeling is an essential *part* of therapy, it does not *in itself* constitute therapy. The other three steps must also be taken, so that you can give yourself orientation and perspective.

A twenty-one-year-old student recently wrote me:

I lay in the clinic after my second suicide attempt, apathetic and numb, and tried to plan my next attempt so that I could not be "saved" to live a life I no longer considered worth living. It was at that time that a friend of mine visited the clinic and gave me a copy of the *Drama.* I flicked through it without interest. Then I suddenly began to read it, even though I couldn't feel anything, perhaps because I was still pumped full of medication. I couldn't stop reading, though. I read the book twice from cover to cover and couldn't put it down, but still didn't know why. Only as I read it for the third time did I begin to cry. I cried and cried, for days on

end, from anger, sadness, and outrage. I wanted to stop taking medication, even though that meant a battle with the
nurses and doctors. For the first time, I wanted to live my
own life. I wanted to feel. "This is easy now," I thought, "all
I need to do is find help"—even though up till then I had
shunned therapy. My decision didn't get me far. I have gone
to several therapists, but they don't understand me. They are
nice and well-meaning, but they seem to be afraid of what I
have to tell them about my childhood. Do you know a therapist who lives near me, who is not afraid to face the truth
about childhood?

Over the years I have received numerous queries of this
kind. And for a long time I helplessly faced the fact that people
often see a new path as they read the *Drama,* a path that makes
sense and that they would like to follow, only to realize that
they cannot pursue it without the appropriate tools. I would
like all of you who read the *Drama* to know that these tools are
now available—that you can help yourself and that your desire
to save your own life and to live it is justified and attainable.
The only things you need are determination, a description of
the therapy, a tape recorder, and time. If you do not have your
own space, you can always turn to the outdoors. People who
live in the city have written to tell me that they have practiced
the therapy in parks or found other places where they can be
alone. The search for the true self just requires inner commit-
ment and the right method. And that method is now available
in *Making Sense of Suffering.*

One young woman wrote of her troubles getting help for her
compulsion to mutilate her body. She had first undergone a
type of body "therapy," which helped her retrieve memories of
having been ritualistically tortured and terrified by her own
parents and other members of a cult. But the body therapist
could not believe that the things she was reporting could actually have happened. The young woman then enrolled in a

clinic, expecting to find more support in the therapeutic group there, only to be faced with even stronger defenses on the part of the psychiatrists and group members, who became hostile to her because her story scared them so much. It was only when she learned to use the Four-Step Method, with the forest as her silent but friendly and reliable witness, that she could express her murderous rage and—by connecting it with the facts of which she was by then aware—recognize how fully justified this rage, this delayed reaction, actually was.

A couple of years later, she wrote:

> How could I expect anybody to believe me? Now I know that what the abusers did to me and to my siblings is more than unbelievable. The word "cruelty" would hardly cover this combination of brainwashing, sadism, shameless perversity, and violence. Because they were so sure that a child would forget everything, they felt secure. This is the reason I am writing you this letter and asking you to use it in your next book. I want to say to every child abuser that no matter how well repression might work, the memories *can* be retrieved if the agonizing feelings are experienced and the truth is eventually admitted. They have to know that even if many authorities and therapists still refuse to believe, others are beginning to recognize that it is a crime to ignore children's reports. Everyone who hurts a child should know that they are risking punishment, now or later. The child's memory can't be buried forever. It can eventually rise up from the darkness of the silent body and from the confusion of repressed feelings into the light of consciousness and can find words to recount the true story and to accuse the perpetrator.

You can find out about Stettbacher's therapy for yourself by reading his description of the method, applying it, and seeing at firsthand the way it works. A sequel to *Making Sense of Suffering* is planned for 1995–96, which you will also be able to use as a guide and accompaniment to self-therapy.

Whether you are prepared to make use of this method will depend on your need, your determination, and your insight. The *Drama* can help you with the insight. It cannot do more; it cannot be a substitute for your therapy. That you will have to follow for yourself. The cells of your body have stored within them the knowledge of what you have been through. Only by listening to them can you discover your own history.

Instead of deceiving your body with alcohol, drugs, and medications, you can listen to it and let its complaints be heard. That is the *first* step, and a very important one, since most of us learned very early in our lives to do the opposite: not to complain. It is not until we learn, however, to face the actual event, to articulate our discomfort, our sensations of body and mind, our concerns and confusion, that we get in touch with ourselves, with what is going on inside us, here and now. The body is an important doorway through which we gain entrance to ourselves. Instead of going on a journey around the world to escape the pain of the wounds inflicted on you, you can stay where you are and, from that vantage point, try to give voice to your feelings. This is the *second* step. You can feel and articulate the pain that was inflicted on you long ago and has been triggered by a present event, and that you have been unconsciously carrying within yourself ever since. In your imagination, you can summon the person who caused you to feel such anger, fear, and outrage. You can look him or her in the face and in an "inner dialogue" describe what you are feeling. The more you practice, the more you will have to say. If fear blocks you, tell your abuser so. Say: "You make me feel so afraid that I cannot utter a single word." Keep saying it, until you fully experience the fear or until it subsides in you, making way for other feelings to surface—like the anger you may feel that, even after all these years, you are still afraid to look that person in the face. In the *third* step you can ask how it is that as a grown man or woman you still feel so threatened and defenseless in even the imaginary presence of this person. In the *fourth* step, you can tell this person how he or she ought to have behaved toward you and enabled you to live without fear, irrational anxieties, or drugs, and without needing to torture yourself or others. This fourth step—finding the repressed need—will help you to come out of the confusion, to see your needs more clearly and find ways to fulfill them, so that you can stop the self-destructive flights you have been engaged in and, at last, learn to live with yourself.

For a long time I traced the strong reactions the *Drama* evoked to the fact that readers made contact with their feelings while reading the book. Today, I believe there is another, deeper cause. (After all, strong feelings can be aroused by reading thrillers or romance novels.) I think that most readers who are affected by the *Drama* somehow feel that it is *their* story, a story they had perhaps repressed completely until then. Their feelings return them to their real foundations, from which they had been alienated as if from something dangerous but which held something familiar after all—their own truth. In the process, they may recapture the hope they had almost given up: the hope that they could discover their real self and live.

I suspect that everyone knows, deep down, that this is the only way to find true health. Inspired by this knowledge, the body will function in an appropriate, life-supporting manner. Sadly, however, this knowledge is continually challenged by the "experts," who do their best to wean patients away from the idea that they can at last possess their true and complete history. As these experts uncritically continue to use the old pedagogical and moralistic vocabulary with which you grew up, they can easily intimidate and discourage you in your search. They can trigger your old fear and your old readiness to adapt. As they often disguise their own fears with pseudopsychological language, they may end up by confusing you. In contrast, the Four Steps and your own body can help you to find clarity and growth. Therapists who refuse even to try this method may be dangerous for you, as they will only aggravate the strong fears you already have.

I wish you determination and tenacity as you begin your journey of self-therapy, especially for this, the initial—and hardest—phase. But with success will come support, confirmation, and the certainty that you are on the right track.

This therapy not only was an exciting journey of personal discovery for me, as it will be for you; it is a precise and viable scientific discovery that will surely have far-reaching implications for our entire society. For the first time a method has been found that enables us to recognize the injuries done to us, evaluate them with our bodies, and then repair them ourselves. In spite of the fact that it is not an easy process, I believe that many will follow it because it offers something that cannot be found anywhere else: our own true stories. In my next book I will describe what happened to me, personally, on this journey of self-discovery.

The function of the *Drama,* however, is to clear a path for *your own journey.* To this end I have undertaken the revision of the old text and have deleted those parts that today appear to me imprecise, superfluous, or misleading—for instance, the word "narcissistic," which I decided to dispense with throughout the book. I have also tried to help the reader sort out the numerous "therapeutic" groups and recovery movements that proliferate in the world today. When I used the word "gifted" in the title, I had in mind neither children who receive high grades in school nor children talented in a special way. I simply meant all of us who have survived an abusive childhood thanks to an ability to adapt even to unspeakable cruelty by becoming numb. Without this ability, without this "gift" offered us by nature, we would not have survived. Others have not. But surviving alone is not enough; it is not the same as being alive. To find the way out of the drama, we will have to realize that each of us was born with the right to be (and to mature as) a feeling and conscious person. Surviving through numbness was not our natural goal; it was a necessity forced on us.

The people who were responsible for us wanted us to be numb, because our consciousness would have challenged their defenses. But for our future we alone are responsible. No one can hinder us now in respecting our crucial needs, in discovering our truth, and in living with it if we choose to do so.

Only after liberation from numbness are we able to recognize, identify, and realize our healthy options of today. The betrayed child has no option other than being a victim. But as adults, we are no longer victims, no matter how much we feel that we are, because we do have other options. One of them is rejecting lies, the lies of others as well as our own, lies that work together with our illusions, blindness, and self-betrayal. The mistreated and neglected child must endure the mistreatment and neglect; she can neither defend herself nor find help if nobody around wants to help. By contrast, the mistreated adult can find laws to protect her when she is no longer numbed and paralyzed by repressed pain.

Under the protection of our truth, of our knowledge and awareness, we are no longer compelled to become perpetrators or to submit to the endless unconscious suffering of being victims or survivors. Slowly we become more and more aware of what it means to be really alive, to love life, and to want to protect it wherever we are charged (and enabled) by nature to do so.

With all my best wishes for your journey,

ALICE MILLER

# Works Cited

Eicke-Spengler, M. 1977. Zur Entwicklung der Theorie der Depression. *Psyche* 31: 1077–1125.

Ganz, H. 1966. *Pestalozzi*. Zurich: Origo.

Hesse, H. 1965. *Demian*. New York: Harper & Row.

—. 1970. *Gesammelte Werke*. Frankfurt: M. Suhrkamp.

—. 1966. "Kindheit und Jugend vor Neunzehnhundert." In *Briefen und Lebenszeugnissen 1877–1895*. Frankfurt: M. Suhrkamp.

—. 1971. "A child's heart." In *Klingsor's last summer*. New York: Harper & Row.

Lavater-Sloman, M. 1977. *Pestalozzi*. Zurich and Munich: Artemis.

Miller, A. 1983. *For your own good: Hidden cruelty in childrearing and the roots of violence*. New York: Farrar, Straus and Giroux.

—. 1984. *Thou shalt not be aware: Society's betrayal of the child*. New York: Farrar, Straus and Giroux, (PB) New American Library; London: Pluto Press.

—. 1986. *Pictures of a childhood: 66 watercolors and an essay*. New York: Farrar, Straus and Giroux. (PB) Meridian/Penguin; London: Virago Press (1995, with a new preface).

—. 1990a. *The untouched key: Tracing childhood trauma in creativity and destructiveness*. New York: Doubleday, (PB) Anchor Press; London: Virago Press.

—. 1990b. *Banished knowledge: Facing childhood injuries.* New York: Doubleday, (PB) Anchor Press; London: Virago Press.

—. 1991. *Breaking down the wall of silence: The liberating experience of painful truth.* New York: Dutton/Penguin.

—. 1993. *Breaking down the wall of silence: The liberating experience of painful truth.* (PB with an essay). New York: Meridian/Penguin; London: Virago Press.

Mueller-Braunschweig, H. 1974. Psychopathologie und Kreativität. *Psyche* 28: 600–654.

Nagara, H. 1967. *Vincent van Gogh.* London: Allen and Unwin.

Stettbacher, J. K. 1991. *Making sense of suffering: The healing confrontation with your past.* New York: Dutton/Penguin; (PB) Meridian/Penguin.

## NOTE TO THE WORKS CITED

To preserve the associative style of the original *Drama* and keep its contents accessible to the lay reader, I have tried not to overload this book with references. Interested professionals can, however, refer for specific topics to the books I have written in the years since the *Drama* was first published:

1. The issue of *manipulation in therapy* is dealt with extensively in *Thou Shalt Not Be Aware*, with specific references to various therapy techniques which I consider to be manipulative.

2. The issue of *manipulation and mistreatment in childhood* is the main theme of *For Your Own Good,* where I also substantiate, with well-known examples, my opinion on the roots of serial crimes, murder, and drug addiction.

3. The goal of the revised version of the *Drama* is above all to make people aware of the fact that it is impossible either to receive or to provide real therapeutic help as long as the personal, emotional confrontation with one's own past is avoided. As the tendency to escape the truth of one's unique history by means of theoretical, religious, pseudo-scientific, and (always) manipulative concepts continues to be very fashionable, I wanted to be as clear

as possible on this point. I hope that my rather broad descriptions of certain "therapies" and the readers' own experience with self-therapy will make them more alert and better able to recognize these misleading concepts on their own, should they be exposed to them in the future.

# *Appendix*

This is a text I wrote in 1984 that has appeared frequently in newspapers. I include it here because it may prove helpful to the reader who has not read my earlier books.

In 1613, when Galileo Galilei presented mathematical proof for the Copernican theory that the earth revolved around the sun and not the opposite, it was labeled "false and absurd" by the Church. Galileo was forced to recant and subsequently became blind. Not until three hundred years later did the Church finally decide to give up its illusion and remove his writings from the Index.

Now we find ourselves in a situation similar to that of the Church in Galileo's time, but for us today much more hangs in the balance. Whether we decide for truth or illusion will have far more serious consequences for the survival of humanity than was the case in the seventeenth century. For some years now, there has been evidence that the devastating effects of the traumatization of children take their inevitable toll on society, leading to inconceivable violence in society and to the repetition of child abuse in the next generation—a phenomenon that we are still forbidden to recognize. This knowledge concerns every single one of us and—if disseminated widely enough—should lead to fundamental changes in society, above all to a halt in the blind escalation of violence. The following points are intended to amplify my meaning:

1. All children are born to grow, to develop, to live, to love, and to articulate their needs and feelings for their self-protection.

2. For their development, children need the respect and protection of adults who take them seriously, love them, and honestly help them to become oriented in the world.

3. When these vital needs are frustrated and children are, instead, abused for the sake of adults' needs by being exploited, beaten, punished, taken advantage of, manipulated, neglected, or deceived without the intervention of any witness, then their integrity will be lastingly impaired.

4. The normal reactions to such injury should be anger and pain; since children in this hurtful kind of environment, however, are forbidden to express their anger and since it would be unbearable to experience their pain all alone, they are compelled to suppress their feelings, repress all memory of the trauma, and idealize those guilty of the abuse. Later they will have no memory of what was done to them.

5. Disassociated from the original cause, their feelings of anger, helplessness, despair, longing, anxiety, and pain will find expression in destructive acts against others (criminal behavior, mass murder) or against themselves (drug addiction, alcoholism, prostitution, psychic disorders, suicide).

6. If these people become parents, they will often direct acts of revenge for their mistreatment in childhood against their

own children, whom they use as scapegoats. Child abuse is still sanctioned—indeed, held in high regard—in our society as long as it is defined as child rearing. It is a tragic fact that parents beat their children in order to escape the emotions stemming from how they were treated by their own parents.

7. If mistreated children are not to become criminals or mentally ill, it is essential that at least once in their life they come in contact with a person who knows without any doubt that the environment, not the helpless, battered child, is at fault. In this regard, knowledge or ignorance on the part of society can be instrumental in either saving or destroying a life. Here lies the great opportunity for relatives, social workers, therapists, teachers, doctors, psychiatrists, officials, and nurses to support the child and to believe him or her.

8. Till now, society has protected the adult and blamed the victim. It has been abetted in its blindness by theories, still in keeping with the pedagogical principles of our great-grandparents, according to which children are viewed as crafty creatures, dominated by wicked drives, who invent stories and attack their innocent parents or desire them sexually. In reality, children tend to blame themselves for their parents' cruelty and to absolve the parents, whom they invariably love, of all responsibility.

9. For some years now, it has been possible to prove, thanks to the use of new therapeutic methods, that repressed traumatic experiences in childhood are stored up in the body and, although remaining unconscious, exert their influence even in adulthood. In addition, electronic testing of the fetus has revealed a fact previously unknown to most adults: A child responds to and learns both tenderness and cruelty from the very beginning.

10. In the light of this new knowledge, even the most absurd behavior reveals its formerly hidden logic once the traumatic

experiences of childhood no longer must remain shrouded in darkness.

11. Our sensitization to the cruelty with which children are treated, until now commonly denied, and to the consequences of such treatment will as a matter of course bring to an end the perpetuation of violence from generation to generation.

12. People whose integrity has not been damaged in child-hood, who were protected, respected, and treated with honesty by their parents, will be—both in their youth and adulthood—intelligent, responsive, empathic, and highly sensitive. They will take pleasure in life and will not feel any need to kill or even hurt others or themselves. They will use their power to defend themselves but not to attack others. They will not be able to do otherwise than to respect and protect those weaker than themselves, including their children, because this is what they have learned from their own experience and because it is *this* knowledge (and not the experience of cruelty) that has been stored up inside them from the beginning. Such people will be incapable of understanding why earlier generations had to build up a gigantic war industry in order to feel at ease and safe in this world. Since it will not have to be their unconscious life-task to ward off intimidation experienced at a very early age, they will be able to deal with attempts at intimidation in their adult life more rationally and more creatively.

# Index